LOYALTY

LOYALTY

Stop unwanted staff turnover, boost engagement, and create lifelong advocates

Zoë Routh

Zoë Routh
zoerouth.com

First published by Inner Compass Australia in March 2018

ISBN 978-0-9944119-6-9

Subjects: Success, Fulfilment, Leadership, Mindset, Motivation, Productivity

Author photograph by Oli Sansom – olisansom.com
Edited by Rebecca Stewart – thegallopingskirt.com
Typesetting, book design and printing – bookbound.com.au

For more information about the author
Zoë Routh
Email: zoe@innercompass.com.au
www.**zoerouth**.com

Disclaimer

Contents

For those who dare to lead,
may you be and keep good company.

INTRODUCTION

Why do good people leave a good organisation?

I have spent the past 30 years working with leaders. I help foster their courage, offer support, act as a sounding board, and ensure that they have the skills and strategy to undertake their own version of climbing Mount Everest. Sometimes this is building a business, changing careers, building better workplace cultures, or bringing more fulfilment to their life and work.

For many business leaders, there is one looming mountain with particular challenges.

It's creating staff loyalty in an age of mobility and fluctuation.

Many leaders are frustrated with the effort they put into staff, only for them to leave to work for a competitor or to strike out on their own. This represents not only the loss of a huge investment, but also experience and corporate knowledge. Some blame the fickleness of younger generations. Others, naïvety or lack of appreciation. "They don't know how good they have it here," was one leader's bitter comment.

Amongst the thousands of people I've worked with, I've never met anyone who lacked the desire to do a good job, make a difference, and enjoy the experience. Most people want to make a contribution and feel their time and effort has value.

If this is a fundamental core desire – for employees, managers, and business owners – why then do things fall apart? If there is goodwill and good intentions, why not loyalty too?

Why do good people leave good jobs?

Some reasons are understandable: a family member needs the worker as primary caregiver, or a personal illness demands focused treatment. Or happier ones such as a pregnancy, supporting a spouse in a promotion and a move to a new city, or the chance for an all-expenses paid trip to travel the world and shadow Elon Musk for a year. Any boss would be happy for their staff member in those circumstances.

What about the avoidable staff departures? I have heard disappointment in leaders' voices when a key staff member hands in their resignation. It's a feeling of resigned chagrin. A grim acceptance; a *fait accompli*; an inevitability. One business owner even said to me, "Don't get too attached to your staff because they'd leave you in a nanosecond for a better opportunity. Loyalty does not count for much."

On the other hand, folks who choose to leave their employer often tell their own story of deep disappointment. They feel somehow let down by the organisation, that they were not treated well, and their expectations were unfulfilled.

Somehow the goodwill and the good intentions on both sides are eroded, leaving guarded pain and frustration. A good employee leaves a good business, and all miss out. Why is it so? Can unwanted staff attrition be avoided? These are the questions that gnaw at so many good employers. It seems to me such a waste for all that talent and energy to be scuppered and for resentment to seep in.

On reflection (after years of hearing these leadership stories), it seems that there has been a fundamental breach in the leadership contract.

As leaders, we have a duty to create the conditions and experiences that allow others in our circle of care to flourish. If we do this right, results follow. And we are fulfilled in return. Over the years, I have worked to articulate what the leadership contract is, what the experiences are that we can create, and how we can maintain them for an engaged and happy workplace. This book is the result.

Loyalty serves as a handbook for you to navigate the complex wilderness of staff interactions and to help create a better workplace. One where people enjoy their work and whom they do it with. This handbook shows you how to build loyalty – the deeply resonant and healthy kind – that will build your team and your business results.

At the end of the day, I want you to feel that you did your best effort and best work, in the company of people you respect and appreciate, and where the feeling is mutual.

Zoë Routh, Canberra, 2018

I believe...

I believe that for leaders in many different organisations and industries, there is almost always something that they could do better. I believe that unwanted staff attrition can be stemmed, and that there is a possible world for leaders...

You wake up in happy anticipation of the day ahead. When you arrive, the workplace is humming with energy and excitement. When one team member comes to see you with a challenge, you work through it carefully together, gently encouraging honest conversation. Another colleague arrives later on, and you encourage him to express his concerns. He is brave enough to confront you on a decision you made that has had a negative impact on morale. Though you are dismayed to discover this, you are grateful for his honesty and thank him for it.

At the end of the day, you reflect on the interactions you've had and observed, and feel a deep sense of gratitude. You hold your staff in deep regard, and every day you seek to make their lives a little better. And you know your staff respect you too. You feel united in your cause with them and feel thankful for all that you experience with them. You go home, feeling satisfied and fulfilled.

It sounds great, doesn't it? Unfortunately, a lot of leaders aren't there yet – leaders who are avoiding what I call 'the conversation no-one wants to have'...

———◆———

"This is my resignation notice."

Jane slid an envelope across the table to Andrew. His brow wrinkled with consternation.

"But why? I thought you were happy here?"

"It's time to move on. I've got opportunities elsewhere. And besides, I've done everything I am capable of here. I'm looking for new challenges."

Silence hung between them like a wet blanket. Andrew could not help feeling he was being let down easily and that there was more to the story.

"I'm really sad to let you go. Is there anything I can do to change your mind? We can look at the budget again and maybe get you some more in your salary package…?"

Jane dug in. "Thanks Andrew. I'm afraid I've made a decision. It's time for me to go." Colour crept up her neck.

"Ok. Thanks for letting me know. Let's talk about handover."

He thought, "Damn this generation! No sense of loyalty. You give them everything they want. More money, more responsibility, more flexibility, a better title, better computers, a gym membership and free lunches, and they *still* leave. No sense of duty or commitment. No appreciation for the hard work and sacrifice that went into making this place good. The grass is always greener with that lot."

Then he felt a tug of doubt. What was he doing – or not doing? All his research said that the manager is why people leave, not because of the organisation. Wasn't he a good leader? How had he failed her? What was he doing wrong?

Everywhere he went Andrew thought, "How bad is it? Have I let things slip? What else is going on I haven't noticed? Is it me? Is it the work? Or is it *them*?"

———◆———

Many leaders like Andrew are confronted when staff, especially good staff, hand in their notice. I've listened to many leaders default to the conclusion that it must be them, the staff. Their excuses unfurl: they weren't a good fit with the culture anyway, 'they don't know how good they have it here', or they'll be hard pressed to find a place as flexible or supportive as this one. The final dismissive conclusion is: "It's this generation! They expect everything on a silver platter. They don't believe in putting the time in. They expect to get to the top just for showing up and gracing us with their presence!"

Some of these conclusions may, in fact, be true. However, if leaders default to these conclusions without rigorous self-assessment, then they are doing themselves a huge disservice. As leaders, we can do better. Some people will leave, and we can't keep everyone in our fold (nor would we want to).

We can, however, be the leaders we would like to follow.

We can create a workplace we love to show up to. We can build relationships where people feel safe and happy at work, fulfilled and thrilled by their work. Whether their time with us is short or long, we can feel satisfied that we did a great job being a steward for their development and advancing the cause of our work. We will know that we have been a great boss and have laid the foundations for lifelong advocates for the work, its people, and its leaders.

I know my 'I believe' vision above is not a utopian fantasy. I know it is possible to create such a workplace. There are straightforward structures, processes, and skills you can develop that can set you, your team, and your organisation up for a successful and prosperous work environment.

My approach in *Loyalty* will focus your efforts on three main principles:

1. Create and maintain a sense of **Tribe.**

2. Enable **Touchpoints** that highlight recognition and appreciation.

3. Increase 'meeting' **Talk** to full-blown leadership conversations.

You have in your hot little hands a pathway to creating enduring leadership satisfaction and an antidote to that most befuddling of conundrums: staff turnover.

Let us begin.

The challenges (and crap) we as leaders need to deal with

Leadership is a tough gig. It takes courage and persistence to navigate the choppy waters of modern business life. What are the chief complaints of some of these captains of industry? They range from the day-to-day grind to the petty complaints of staff, the looming pressure from board members to the shifting sands of the forces of change.

Unappreciative staff

From lunches out to Thursday night drinks, bonus payments, staff retreats, even overseas conferences, leaders feel they do a lot to provide good conditions for their employees. When these become an expectation for staff, however, it can be unsettling. This is when 'they don't know how good they've got it here' starts to creep in. Staff expect these rewards to be an integral part of their employment conditions, while business leaders feel that they fail to appreciate how much of an effort it took to put these experiences together.

Staff drama

"Work would be so easy if it weren't for staff and customers."

Working with people is the number one challenge I hear about from leaders, no matter the industry or sector. Many experience it as a necessary evil of leadership duties, and long for the bliss of shutting the door and sailing in delightful solitude while staff storms rage on the other side. Staff dramas are diverse: from petty disagreements to more fractious experiences like harassment or theft. Leaders also know that if they don't deal with these issues quickly and well, they can easily turn into something far more problematic. With staff drama, the culture is at risk. This can lead to staff churn.

Results pressure

It seems like expectations for business leaders have multiplied. With income targets increased, budgets slashed, and expectations of program service delivery increasing, they stare down this double barrel, wondering if they can pull the rabbit of out of the proverbial hat. All while maintaining a cool, calm, and collected air.

Relevancy and currency

Volatility and rapid rates of change sharpen the threat of business disturbance. We hear stories of Uber shaking the taxi industry cage, how Amazon spells the end of retail in Australia, how electric cars will kill off the petrol industry, or how Bitcoin will bring down banking and commerce as we know it. These huge change surges are leaving a dark wake of uncertainty. Business leaders are understandably wary at best, trembling in anxiety at worst.

Less time for the 'big picture'

The pace of work is so fast and expectations around results so elevated that everything seems urgent and important. Business leaders have trouble finding the time and space to do quality 'big picture' thinking beyond the immediate 12-month reporting cycle. And if they do somehow manage to carve out some space for elevated thinking, they find themselves adrift in the possibilities. They often lack the thinking systems and filters they need to apply to the complexity that they are swimming in.

Impostor syndrome

This is such a universal concern, no matter the experience or level of leader. I have yet to work with a leader who did not have a tremor of self-doubt somewhere in their leadership make-up. This is the paradox of growth: to be better and more capable, we need to tackle things we have not tried before. Any new endeavours carry the risk of failure and disappointment.

The more complex a role, the harder it is to quantify impact and lay claim to results. It is harder to prove that your job as a leader is making a difference. This creates its own atmosphere of risk, and many will reason, "If I can't prove I am making a difference, then there is no insulation against those who do not like or support me, for whatever reason." This lack of security can have a destabilising effect on the most experienced leader.

Fear of a 'legacy lost'

Leaders are often fearful of the end result. They say, "I'm scared of not finishing my career and not fulfilling my potential. That I could have done more than I did. That I fell short of what I was capable of." Of all the fears, the fear of living a life with potential unrealised is perhaps the most paralysing. It's always the fear of failure that keeps us from exploring that potential.

Showcase
Outward Bound and beyond

While I was leading groups at Outward Bound, one of my top trainers resigned.

He came in to meet with me, acting a little shy. He wanted to let me know he was leaving. He was off to explore new experiences in a related industry: a field officer for the Antarctic expedition. It was a great opportunity! He was going to learn and develop new skills that we could not offer.

I was pleased for him. And inwardly crestfallen. He had such talent! He was so reliable! I could delegate anything and knew it would be delivered better than I could have done. He had resilience, courage, initiative, conviction, and insightfulness. He was well respected and admired. Now he was going. I felt like someone had chiselled a portion of my three-legged stool to a ragged stump. I was off-balance and scrambling.

In short, I felt let down. In reality, this was just the feeling of having to pick up the pieces and keep going. Departing staff members create a void that needs to be filled – often by colleagues or their supervisors. A lot of disappointment about staff leaving comes back to personal survival. The 'once you go this means more work for me' feeling.

Unexpected and unwanted staff turnover is destabilising and can knock the wind out of your sails.

Sometimes the will to explore these hazards is limited by courage, sometimes by lack of support, and often through lack of knowledge or a sound strategy. After all, if you set out to climb Mount Everest without doing any training or knowing anything about mountaineering, there is a 100 per cent chance of failure.

Let's go through the steps to navigating the troubled waters of staff engagement and come through it with confidence. In every chapter of *Loyalty*, I outline the specific skills you need and give you the actions you can take.

The 'Implement' section in each chapter helps you take what you learn and apply it to your own context. My intention is that through this book you will gain a deeper insight into people and learn the practical steps you need to improve relationships and the atmosphere at work. This is the first critical step in building long-lasting loyalty with your team.

The benefits and pitfalls of loyalty

What is it, what's expected, and why it goes wrong

We all think we know what loyalty is. When someone is committed to an organisation and sticks with us through thick and thin, that shows loyalty. When someone has our back and jumps in to support us in troubled times, that is loyalty.

As employers, if someone resigns and goes to a competitor, we feel that they are being disloyal. Sometimes loyalty can be hazardous: we sacrifice our own interests to serve others or we act unethically to protect a person or organisation out of misguided loyalty.

Loyalty is a complex emotional and behavioural contract. Some of it has legal ramifications. If we are to expect and grow loyalty with our staff, it's important that we know what it means, and what its limitations and dangers are. There are three components of loyalty that we need to explore before we take action with our teams: What is loyalty? When does loyalty become unhealthy, and why? And what turns a loyal person disloyal?

1. What is loyalty?

Loyalty is an alliance to a person, group, or cause that includes particular types of behaviours. These behaviours include commitment, duty, and responsibility.

Commitment is the willingness to give your time and energy to something that you believe in. It's a promise that you keep and activities that require time and energy away from other priorities, such as work that keeps you from family, and family obligations that interrupt work. *Duty* is something that you undertake as part of your work role, or something that you feel is the right thing to do (this could be the duty to report sexual harassment in the workplace, or the duty to notify the police when you see a robbery). *Responsibility* is when you are in a position of authority over someone and have to ensure that particular things are done. A manager has a responsibility to make sure that their team delivers on its work assignments by certain dates.

Loyalty is our decision to play a part in something we believe in. We embrace our role as part of the overall narrative of a story that inspires us. It's personal action in a purposeful context. It's at once deeply personal and global in its reach.

A brief history of the different types of loyalty

Swearing fealty

In earlier ages, swearing loyalty to the lord of the group or land was an oath taken by a subject to swear allegiance and loyalty to his lord. In return, the lord promised to protect and remain loyal to his subject. The ceremony usually included an act of homage, such as kneeling and offering hands in prayer and complete submission. It was a contract with mutual benefits. As a more sophisticated concept, loyalty has evolved beyond commitment to one's tribe to devotion to a cause, country, group, or person.

Loyalty to one's country

We owe allegiance to our country, and as citizens agree to obey its laws and support its interests. These are part of the rights and responsibilities of a citizen. Citizenship ceremonies even include swearing oaths of allegiance.

Loyalty to one's spouse

Wedding vows are a type of oath and have their origins in early Roman times, from 17 BC onwards. The lower classes had free marriages and agreed to keep the vow of marriage. Wealthier Romans would sign documents listing property rights to declare their marriage publicly, thereby legalising it. This was the beginning of the official recording of marriage (and has become a very lucrative profession for divorce lawyers ever since!).

Loyalty to a brand

Apple customers are known to be a bit fanatical. They believe in the quality of the products, appreciate the origin story of its founders, and admire its development within the marketplace. Brand fans love the story and love what associating with the brand says about them.

Loyalty to a celebrity

Celebrities also have fans. Take Roger Federer for example. Even when he loses a game, fans appreciate his sportsmanship, his gentleman-like manners, and his commitment to his family and the sport of tennis. His values and style resonate with who his fans aspire to be, and what they value.

More intense forms of loyalty

Devotion is profound dedication. This can be to a person, a religious faith, or a practice. Patriotism is the sentiment of feeling love for your country (whether born there or now a citizen) and believing it better than others. Martyrdom is the highest of all stakes in loyalty: dying for your cause or country. We see this kind of self-sacrifice in military institutions from earliest times. Roman generals made a vow of 'devotion' to pledge their lives on the battlefield in exchange for victory.

A pledge to higher principles of honour and protection of Rome, or to the moral code of duty, guided this kind of action. The idea of pledging of one's life is a core principle of sacrifice that is at the heart of military duty and something we honour on days like ANZAC Day and Remembrance Day. We honour the commitment of millions of individuals to uphold the values and the way of life of their nation and cause.

2. When does loyalty become unhealthy, and why?

So far these are all healthy expressions of loyalty in its various forms. Unhealthy expressions of loyalty are those that become extreme and obsessive. Fans become fanatics. The enthusiastic support of person, country, or cause becomes unreasonable and uni-focal. A fan sees competition as bringing out the best in each team, while a fanatic sees competition as the means to crush opponents. Why? To distinguish between healthy and blind loyalty we ask:

Is the loyalty focused on positive gains for the greatest good?

Or is the loyalty focused on positive gains to the exclusion of others?

Healthy loyalty wants success for one's own team; unhealthy loyalty wants the success of one's own team at the expense of all others. This is the difference between being a fan and defaulting to fanaticism. Fans are those who are keenly enthusiastic about their chosen team, sport or religion. Fanaticism changes this to the denigration of others whose beliefs are different to one's own.

Healthy loyalty is inclusive and supportive; unhealthy loyalty is exclusive and destructive.

As leaders, we need to be vigilant about discouraging unhealthy loyalty. Unhealthy loyalty is based on the premise of scarcity, that there is not enough to go around and that we must claim and control what we can. It's fear based, and no longer relevant in a society that is well resourced and offers ample opportunity.

Showcase
Loyalty in *House of Cards*

The Netflix TV series *House of Cards* is the riveting story of fictional politician Frank Underwood and his manipulations to reach the US Presidency. He is shown to be ruthless, even committing murder amongst his other sins, to forward his ambition.

Underwood's use of loyalty as a weapon is the very worst form of blind loyalty. It demands loyalty to Underwood's directive, above and beyond all other principles. This surfaces in the first season where Underwood seeks to manipulate Congressman Russo for a political outcome.

Underwood exploits Russo's alcoholism and weakens his sobriety through various constructed political and circumstantial pressures.

Russo caves and drinks, and is caught for drunk driving charges, a situation Underwood orchestrated. Underwood offers to have the charges 'go away' in return for loyalty. Their conversation puts Russo in an impossible position.

Russo: What is it you want?

Underwood: Your absolute, unquestioning loyalty.

Russo: Always.

Underwood: Do not misunderstand what I mean by 'loyalty'.

Russo is torn. Unable to pledge blind loyalty, he is prepared to sacrifice his own political career to cleanse his conscience and reveal Underwood as a manipulator. Seeing the threat, Underwood murders him under the guise of a remorseful suicide by car exhaust fumes after a drunken binge.

Personality cults demand this kind of loyalty. Adolf Hitler is perhaps the most famous. Others include Muammar Gaddafi and Saddam Hussein. The danger in excessive loyalty is when it becomes exclusive and antagonistic towards others and when it overrides other key values. At the extreme end of things, this includes loyalty to a person or cause above respect for human life.

3. What turns a loyal person disloyal?

Disloyalty is not supporting someone that you should support because of previous commitments, duties, or responsibilities. What causes someone to shirk these? First, let's take a look at some of the forms of disloyalty.

Personal disloyalty

Backstabbing is when someone says harmful things about us when we are not there to defend ourselves. We can add malicious gossip to this category as well. Adultery is sex between a married man or woman and someone else that he or she is not married to. The causes of this kind of disloyalty are varied: from escaping an unsatisfactory relationship, to living out fantasies, to boredom, to a need for a change, to reassurance. Breaking promises is a form of disloyalty, a form of betrayal where one person expects a behaviour or commitment and it is revoked or ignored.

National disloyalty

Treason is the crime of showing no loyalty to your own country, especially by helping its enemies or trying to defeat or remove its government. A high-profile example of this in recent years is National Security Agency contractor Edward Snowden. In 2013, Snowden was concerned about over-reaching digital surveillance of citizens, and leaked details of the NSA's top-secret PRISM data collection program.

Showcase
Edward Snowden – treason or loyalty?

On June 14, 2013, United States federal prosecutors filed a criminal complaint against Edward Snowden. They charged him with theft of government property and two counts of violating the Espionage Act[1]. He escaped first to Hong Kong and then to Russia, where he was granted a one-year temporary political asylum visa, then a three-year residency permit, but not permanent political asylum.

The Snowden case raises concerns about breach of loyalty to one's organisation and to one's country. The information he disclosed was damaging to the agency, as it revealed their surveillance secrets. It was potentially damaging to the USA, as it also revealed how surveillance was handled – and therefore could be avoided – making it easier for enemies of America to operate without detection on American soil.

Snowden maintains that his motivation was to highlight that American security should not come at the cost of all privacy. He felt that that the method was likely unconstitutional, and that it violated citizen rights. He reported policy or legal issues related to spying programs to more than ten officials, but as a contractor had no legal avenue to pursue further whistleblowing[2].

---

1 'Edward Snowden', *Wikipedia, The Free Encyclopaedia* (accessed 22 January 2018).

2 A. Petersen, 'Snowden: I raised NSA concerns internally over 10 times before going rogue', *The Washington Post*, 7 March 2014.

Military disloyalty

Mutiny is rebellion against an authority figure, with the purpose of changing, opposing, or overthrowing that authority. Desertion is when a person leaves the armed forces without permission. A breach of commitment or duty can sometimes be attributed to one's own personal drive for survival, overriding any sense of commitment to the collective.

This is particularly evident in cases of desertion. Soldiers, under an unrelenting barrage of attacks and atrocious conditions, simply reach breaking point. In some cases, soldiers desert because all the others in their unit had been killed and their own death seemed inevitable[3]. Many mutinies and loyalties are attributed by the dissenters to their leaders and the organisation, who they say were not fulfilling their commitments as leaders.

Showcase
Yorkshire Regiment Soldiers jailed for a sit-in protest

In 2014, on an exercise in Kenya, 16 men from the 1st Battalion the Yorkshire Regiment sat on the floor when ordered to stand to attention. After pleading guilty to disobeying a lawful command (a sentence that carries ten years' imprisonment), 15 were sentenced to detention and two were dismissed from the army.

According to the inquiry, the protest was as a result of grievances with their captain and sergeant. The testimony tells us that the soldiers felt they were being "led by muppets" and that their boss and his second-in-command got drunk before a key training march in Wales.

When they completed a 16-mile march in full kit across the Brecon Beacons, the men were furious to find the pair sleeping off their hangovers instead of ceremoniously welcoming their soldiers across the finishing line. They felt their leaders had violated a moral code: not looking out for their men or showing regard for their welfare.

---

3   C. Glass, 'Breaking point: Why do soldiers desert?' *HistoryNet*, 19 April 2017.

The issue for the army is obvious: if they allowed such examples of insubordination to go unpunished, it sets the scene for future protests. Army discipline and following orders is one of the critical practices that ensure army effectiveness: challenging a leader's command in the heat of a battle can cause many casualties. This is why it is so incredibly difficult to challenge authority. One principle may override another, causing overall destabilisation of the organisation.

Mutineers come face to face with their loyalties, but which principle rules the others? For leaders, the critical insight is not to be a 'muppet'.

Loyalty is essentially an alignment of values and purpose between an individual and another entity, be that a person, cause, country, idea, or way of life. There is an expected return for that loyalty, be it protection, civic rights, or consistency. Each context of loyalty has an official and moral code attached to it.

The challenge for contemporary workplaces is that employers' expectations of loyalty itself remain centred on longevity. Employers feel that loyalty means sticking with the organisation and its leadership through thick and thin. Expectations of employees and the work context itself has shifted. So too should our concept and practice of loyalty, and the leadership contract that goes with it.

The new context of staff loyalty

What has changed in workplaces?

How we experience work and workplaces has changed significantly over the last ten years, even if our expectations of staff loyalty have not. We must first consider the factors at play in shaping new attitudes, and what it means for us as leaders.

The plague of disengagement

Gallup has one of the most extensive global research databases on employee engagement. Since 2000 when Gallup started measuring it, the results have not varied much: roughly 33 per cent of employees are engaged at work. That means that two out of three employees are *not* engaged. This is the statistic for US companies. Globally it's worse, at 15 per cent[4].

In 2016, Gallup released the results of surveying 82,000 work units worldwide on employee engagement. It found that the work units with the highest levels of engagement delivered nearly four times the business results. In other words, engaged employees mean tangible benefits to your business[5]. Thus if your business follows the same trend as that of nearly two-thirds of other businesses, it means that you are losing money, effort, and results, hand over fist.

What this means for you: Employee engagement is a critical strategic lever that needs to be pulled. It cannot be left to chance. Designing experiences and workplaces that people want to belong to and are proud to advocate for is one of our key leadership responsibilities.

4   L. Emond, '2 reasons why employee engagement programs fall short', *Gallup News*, 15 August, 2017.

5   J. Harter, 'Moneyball for business: Employee engagement meta', *Gallup News*, 31 May, 2016.

The 'gig economy' fallacy

The gig economy was meant to liberate the enslaved masses. With the lure of autonomy – being your own boss, setting your own hours, managing your own routines on your terms from whenever and wherever you wanted – and due to the advent of technology (mobile tech, easily accessible and affordable or cheap Wi-Fi), hordes of workers were meant to leave full-time employment to be captains of their own ship.

Reality is a lot harsher. There is a significant difference in mindset and work requirements between being an employee and being an independent contractor.

Most workers still favour the relative (perhaps imagined) security of regular paid employment. The promise of stability and security is implied: I show up to work, you give me a regular pay cheque. But an independent contractor has to hustle. They have to seek out the work as well as do it. They have to manage the infrastructure of the work as well as do the work itself. The relationship to risk is quite significantly different. And with the promise of the gig economy's alleged freedoms, its initial popular insurgence has meant that competition has driven prices quite low. It's harder to make a living as a contractor, unless you develop exceptional and deep expertise. This requires grit and persistence. This kind of life is not for everyone, however it sits there as an alluring alternative to the naive and uninitiated. Staff are often keen to use this as a bargaining chip.

What this means for you: We need to create employee experiences that combine the best aspects of the consultant life with the benefits of regular paid employment. Lack of autonomy and appreciation can drive even the most reluctant employee to test the waters as a contractor.

Digital nomads

Mobile technology has made it easier for workers to have holidays and keep on top of work. This allows greater flexibility for families when planning breaks: they can book trips during school weeks instead of lumping in with the masses. Kids can do homework remotely, and parents can stay connected to what is going on in the office. This makes for an interesting impact on the nature of holidays. Getting downtime when it is so easy to check email requires strong discipline.

The concern for work imposing on personal time resonates with an email-overloaded workforce. In 2014, a false report stated that France had passed legislation banning emails after 6pm. Some thought it audacious and others brilliant, but there was never any such legislation. There was a labour agreement in the high-tech industry for autonomous or contracted employees whose agreements composed days worked, not hours worked, so the 35-hour work rule did not apply. There is no reference to a 6pm cut-off[6]. The false story flags the dangers of a digital life: no sensible boundaries.

The story illustrates the freedoms that mobile and easy access to Wi-Fi have allowed us, which also means the ability to work from anywhere, anytime. For example, I wrote a chapter of this book in a café in Brisbane, while waiting for a client meeting. I've recorded podcasts in my car and videos on a mountaintop, and written newsletters on planes. While the dangers of constantly working are ever-present, what it has also allowed is the exploration of lifestyle by design. I can work and live anywhere in the world, while still making a living.

Showcase
Finance expert, entrepreneur, and author of *Get Rich Slow*, Sarah Riegelhuth

In 2017, I interviewed Sarah for the *Zoë Routh Leadership Podcast*. This is an excerpt from the transcript[7].

Zoë: I have been chasing Sarah around the globe, she's been in the US and now she's ended up in the Philippines and we're just having a chat about how she runs her world. She is originally Australian and hasn't spent that much time there. Sarah, can you tell us about how you run your life right now with your business?

---

6 Charlemagne, 'Not what it seemed', *The Economist*, 14 April 2014.

7 Z. Routh, 'Sarah Riegelhuth Interview', audio blog post, Zoë Routh Leadership Podcast, 17 January 2018.

Sarah: I'm a bit of a nomad or a gypsy, as my family like to call me. I do like to be able to work from anywhere. In the first few years in my business that wasn't possible, or I probably didn't think it was possible, so I didn't set it up that way. But about three or four years ago, I decided that it was, so I started changing the business to be more flexible and more remote. This was great for both me and my team. They really liked the flexibility, they liked being able to work from home, and it allowed us to then start hiring people from all over the world, as well as from Australia. It has been really fun and exciting to experience the amazing talent and diversity that exists in the world.

Bringing people into the business from different cultures is really fun as well. And it has challenges, but we have a good time around that. So we've successfully transitioned to a fully flexible, fully remote team. That allowed me the freedom to get back into living a lifestyle where I can spend time in different parts of the world.

What this means for you: We need to be mindful of the health traps of being constantly accessible and constantly on, and create boundaries for ourselves and our staff. We also need to keep in mind how we might create experiences that allow our team members to have a version of being digital nomads without having to leave the comfort and safety of the employee fold.

Automation, globalization, and collaboration, and its effect on young people's careers

University students are studying while the jobs they will end up in don't even exist yet. The idea of building a career in one solid area of interest or skill is gone. In a 2015 report commissioned by the Foundation for Young Australians, research showed that 58 per cent of students and 71 per cent of vocational education students are on a career path that may disappear or be fundamentally rerouted[8].

A 'portfolio career' is where we can move from one area of expertise to another. Technology and access to learning and development means that we can be nimble and adapt to follow our interests and move on to something new. Conversely, if we are not proactive, we

---

8   The Foundation For Young Australians, 'The New Work Order report', FYA, 2015.

might find ourselves without a role as automation makes our job redundant.

Job security has been replaced with job fulfilment. We have moved out of the survival mode that drove our grandfathers into loyalty of obedience and tenancy of endurance, and we are now moving into exploration and fulfilment mode. Maslow's Hierarchy of Needs [9] – of food, security, and shelter – have been more than well met after the Industrial Revolution. The internet age unleashed the revolution of discovery and exploration.

What this means for you: Discovery and fulfilment are now primary drivers for many top executives. If we are not focusing on developing our people, we risk losing our best and brightest.

The matrix organisation

The matrix organisation is on the rise. This is one where people work on projects, on various teams, and across many different divisions. We see this with the growth of agile methodology, which is a quick prototyping of products with an assembled team led by a scrum master [10]. The agile approach promises freedom and flexibility, and nimble, explosive development to test and iterate quickly. What it can mean for workers is often confusion, competing priorities, conflicting reporting lines, fuzzy accountability, and diffused responsibility.

What this means for you: We need to hone our communication and conversation skills. We need to develop a cadence and system of visible accountability. Lack of transparency and poor communication will be our downfall in these situations! Uncertainty and overload will drive our staff to seek out a more stable, clear-cut environment.

Generational expectations

Ever since the Gen Y cohort jumped into the workforce, Gen Xers and

---

9   A.H. Maslow, 'A theory of human motivation', *Psychological Review*, 50 (4), 1943, pp. 370–96.

10   A. Kepshire, 'Growth of Agile', *LinkedIn Pulse*, 28 April 2017. This is an easy-to-read explanation of agile that explains the methodology.

Baby Boomers have struggled to accommodate them. They seemed like a strange new breed.

Get X started their work career without the internet and after a difficult recession. They had had ideas of job security hammered into them by their Baby Boomer parents, who had had it hammered into them by their traumatised parents who had survived the Great Depression and two World Wars. When Gen X started work, there was no widespread internet. Email did not appear on the scene until the mid-1990s, and mobile tech a decade later, when many were in their mid-thirties. Gen X scrambled to keep up.

Get Y slid gleefully into the world, coddled by parents determined to protect their offspring from the treatment they had copped from their own harsh and critical parents. The wanted to do things right for their kids, and they lavished them with praise and encouragement, instilling the belief that everything is possible. Educators taught them about the ills of pollution and corporate greed, to encourage sustainability and earth-friendly practices, and to bolster student self-esteem. When a twenty-something entered the workforce in the early-2000s, they were awash with confidence, conviction, and expectation. They believed meritocracy, not longevity, was a key principle of work performance and recognition.

As a result, they are maligned for their sense of entitlement, over-reaching ambition, lack of respect for elders and experience, and brash arrogance. Some of this may be true. However, there is an energy, a nimbleness and adaptability that Gen Y folks have that their older colleagues do not.

And what of Gen Z? These are the world's first digital natives. They grew up with mobile technology, consider Wi-Fi to be a basic human need, and do not let their mobile phone leave their side, morning or night. 9/11, the terrorist attack that brought down the World Trade Centre and nearly annihilated the Pentagon, happened before they were born.

What does Gen Z expect in the workplace? By all accounts, they are far more pragmatic than their Gen Y siblings. They observed what the Global Financial Crisis did to their parents and grandparents, and the ensuing challenge to corporate greed and the perils of unchecked capitalism. The rise of demands for transparency from leadership was a result. They have seen and heard the stories of failed leadership time and again: corporate salaries 200 times those of workers, the wars that go on endlessly in Afghanistan and Iraq, the bloody and horrendous atrocities in Sudan, the blatant hypocrisy and moral corruption, including rampant sexual harassment and abuse in large organisations.

Is it any wonder that Gen Z is cynical and world weary? The have been told the world is theirs. The world may be their oyster, but it's highly unlikely they'll find a pearl inside. They'll play the game, but they'll play it steeped in caution.

What this means for you: With so many bad examples of leadership and with so much scrutiny, the onus is on leaders to create an alternative. To be the bright and shining light where people love to come to work, feel challenged and appreciated, and go home excited for the next day. We can create businesses and workplaces that are oases for purpose-driven, heart-centred people. We can model what is possible if we create work worth doing, in a place where we feel we belong, and are growing and appreciated. We can create a bubble and beacon of hope against the surge of corruption and fear and negativity.

The end of the 'company man'

A workable definition for contemporary loyalty

Over the last 100 years, the work landscape has changed in a breathtaking way. At the turn of the 20th century, industrialisation was taking hold, and one-industry towns faced a prosperous future. The company man was a worker who, once employed by one of the big industry businesses, was set for life. He was assured of a regular pay cheque, a pension, and a gold watch after years of faithful service.

The term 'company man' evolved during the union movement, when union members were striking to demand better conditions. Those who refused to strike were called company men because they were more loyal to the company than they were to their fellow workers. Today, the manufacturing conditions that gave birth to the company man and the union movement have largely disappeared for many industries.

Rural towns in Australia that rode the mining boom are facing similar challenges, as are the former manufacturing towns in the US that are turning into ghost towns. Once the set-up phase for operations has finished, workers' contracts are terminated. Their drift back to the cities in search of more work has left these communities reeling as inflated housing prices come crashing down.

This volatility means that many businesses need to be nimble and responsive. Job security is no longer on offer in exchange for employee loyalty. Companies seek to protect themselves from promises they cannot keep, and employees start shoring up their options. These are not the conditions for generating the kind of company loyalty employees used to expect.

Loyalty used to be about longevity of service. It used to be about sticking with the job through thick and thin. It used to be about feeling secure and stable, in the bosom of the parental patron.

Loyalty to one's workplace

A common law that imposes a duty of loyalty and fidelity upon all employees is largely summarised in employment contracts. For employees with financial duties, this encompasses their social position of trust and confidentiality. With confidential information, the duty of fidelity says an employee may not use that information to the detriment of their organisation. For public servants, they have an overriding duty to the public that supersedes commitment to the employer. This is meant to encourage disclosing information that may damage the public service, but is in the best interest of the public at large[11].

In Quebec in Canada, it is interesting to note there are workplace laws in place that explicitly govern employee loyalty. On the Canadian equivalent of the Fair Work Ombudsman website, the law states that:

"The law in Quebec requires an employee to be loyal towards his employer. This means that an employee must:

- Be honest with his employer while he works for him
- Use good judgment in his role as an employee
- Put the interests of his employer above his own
- Protect confidential information".[12]

Confidential information includes trade secrets, client lists, company financial information, and business strategies.

These same principles apply to professional conduct here in Australia. Employment in Australia is governed by the Fair Work Act 2009. It comprises a number of responsibilities and entitlements for employees that include flexible working arrangements and fairness at work, and prevents discrimination against employees. These are often backed up by including non-compete clauses in employment contracts that prevent individuals from competing directly with former employers within a certain region and/or for a certain period of time. These are

---

11   'Overview of current secrecy laws', *Australian Law Reform Commission* (accessed 22 January 2018).

12   'Being loyal to your employer', *educaloi.qu.ca*, (accessed 31 January 2018).

the duties, commitments, and responsibilities of today's employee.

It says nothing about loyalty.

Where is the emotional investment? Where is the pride in one's job? Is contemporary company loyalty even possible? I believe it is. It just looks different.

The missing link: Loyalty to one's employees

Workplace loyalty is still a reciprocal arrangement, but the terms have changed. The leadership contract looks quite different. We know the value of loyalty: people have got your back, they go above and beyond to get the job done well and done right, there is pride in the result, satisfaction in the work, and joy in the process. It's fulfilling and fun. So how do we create that when uncertainty is rife, conditions unstable, and opportunities for development are few?

Loyalty is no longer longevity. Loyalty is no longer uni-focal. Loyalty is not enduring service. Loyalty is advocacy of a purpose. Loyalty is commitment to community. Loyalty is lifetime service to vision.

Loyalty is less about security and more about meaning.

The expectation is to have lifelong advocates, not indentured servants. We know that an employee's time with us may be shorter rather than longer. But in exchange, if we do our job right as leaders, we will have an army of supporters whose reach extends well beyond their original circles. Our jobs as leaders then become about creating the environment and experiences that foster meaning and belonging.

Showcase
Creating loyalty as advocacy

'David' has been the Executive Director at a rural industry association since 2006, ten years after he first joined the organisation. Though he has stayed with the business longer than many, he does not see loyalty as longevity. He sees advocacy as the best form of loyalty.

As part of its mandate to its levy payers and its government agency remit, the organisation invests in leadership development across the agricultural sector. Unlike many others, David does not see ROI in its people development programs as dependent on the number of years the people stay employed in the industry. He believes that a good return is creating more effective leaders who advocate for the seafood industry, no matter what industry they end up in. Ultimately, he sees loyalty as an expression of advocacy, especially if it is delivered through better leadership. He holds the cause of better leadership as the reason for investment, not an exchange for a period of service.

It's a gamble, of course. It's hard to measure advocacy as a sensible return to stakeholders, and it can raise more than a few eyebrows if a huge scholarship for a leadership development program results in someone leaving the industry to work in a different sector. What quantifiable effect or benefit can there be? It comes back to how you define loyalty and what are reasonable (perhaps realistic) expectations.

The workplace environment has changed significantly, and so too have the expectations of employees. Expectations of loyalty have not changed, and they need to. We need to focus more on what we can do as employers to create environments and experiences that set us up for success, regardless of how long people might stay with us.

What if we worried less about what employees might do, and focused instead on what we are doing in the workplace? We need to focus on our sphere of influence. As leaders, we can create the environment and experiences that build loyalty. This is the kind of loyalty that is based on mutual respect and commitment to a common cause, which endures beyond the individual's actual tenure in the workplace.

It takes a shift to focus on environment and experiences. It needs a shift in mindset towards one of abundance. It invites the belief that regardless of what employees ultimately choose to do, you know that you've done the best job possible and created the best workplace, one you are proud of. Only then have you set yourself up for the best chance of success, including creating lifelong fans.

Let's get you the skills you need to create the experiences you'll enjoy so that you can reap the rewards you want.

The path to Loyalty

The 'Loyalty Ladder'

STATE	RESULT	ATTRITION unwanted turnover	ANTIDOTE	ENERGY INVESTED ENERGY RETURNED
BOUNDLESS	LOYALTY We are inspired	5% or less	Tribe: BELONGING	1:5
CONSIDERED	ENGAGEMENT We've earned this	10%	Touchpoints: GROWTH	1:3
RESPONSIVE	ENTITLEMENT We deserve more	15%	Touchpoints: APPRECIATION	5:1
REACTIVE	MUTINY They owe us	30%	Talk: ACCOUNTABILITY	10:1
AGGRESSIVE	DESERTION I'm out of here	40%	Talk: LISTEN	10:0

Read the model from the bottom up. On the Loyalty Ladder, where does your team sit?

Each state and its result in your team is described below.

STATE 1: Aggressive

Result: Desertion

Like military desertions, this is when things are bad. No one buys your message and they are leaving in droves. The individual feels that there is no longer a place for them, that the organisation is out of step with their own desires, and they no longer feel supported or safe. Desertion is a survival choice.

There is no point trying to convince them to stay. The best we can do is to listen and hear what people say about why they are leaving. Significant turnover is definitely a time to pause and explore the conditions that created it. People who are leaving are in survival mode and feel under siege. Their amygdala (the fight and flight mechanism of the brain) is activated, and no rational discussion will occur at this point. We need to surrender to their decision and support them as best we can. And listen to what they have to say.

Listening is a critical skill in the 'Talk' component. It takes courage to hear what dissenters and deserters have to say. Some things are outside our control. We may have had change imposed upon us by external forces. And there may be feedback that helps us make the next moves: what could be improved, what we might influence, where we may have misunderstood or made a misstep. The bravest leaders seek feedback, however painful, because it is the gateway to growth.

STATE 2: Reactive

Result: Mutiny

If we have mutineers on board, we are in for a world of pain. Strong action is required. Let's first be cautious, as mutineers are not usually malicious. They may potentially be misguided or even misinformed. If that is the case, then communication is the starting point. This requires the skills of 'Talk'. We should be focused on accountability, listening for the contributing factors that led to the mutinous climate, including our own actions and inactions.

The sense of being wronged, that the organisation 'owes' them something, is often coupled with a righteous sense of wanting to put things right. Mutinous actions potentially have a rich goldmine of energy and information to be mined by the leader. Mutineers can often shed light on decisions that had unwanted and unintended results, to which leaders may have been oblivious.

In *Mutiny and Its Bounty: Leadership Lessons from the Age of Discovery* [13], Patrick Murphy and Ray Coye examine various mutinies from the seafaring Age of Discovery to assert that mutiny is an entrepreneurial force. In modern organisations, mutinies occur when there is a gap between the values of what the leadership espouses and what the workers value. Often a decision that threatens the workers' values was made unintentionally, such as one that threatens a sense of belonging or growth opportunities, or disrupts operating systems. Mutinies arise when the common goal of organisational success is perceived as being at risk with the leader. 'Successful' mutinies can result in the organisation getting back on track and improving its processes. Sometimes this means removal of the leader, sometimes it means improvement in the leadership. Ousting the leader is not always the primary objective; safeguarding the business is.

Business leaders and employers need to pay attention to mutinous behaviour and comments. It's often the canary in the coal mine. It may be that we need to communicate a vision better, adjust a decision, or even address some of our own leadership shortfalls. Courageous accountability and transparency is the intervention required, from the leader first. We will need to implement the listening skills of 'Talk', then consider how aligned our actions are with our sense of 'Tribe'. Rigorous self-assessment is required.

---

13   P. J. Murphy and R.W. Coye, *Mutiny and Its Bounty: Leadership Lessons from the Age of Discovery*, New Haven and London, Yale University Press, 2013.

STATE 3: Responsive

Result: Entitlement

This is a thorny issue. How do we contend with the sense of 'I deserve it?' These individuals have a strong sense that something is owed to them. They feel that effort versus return is out of balance. On the other hand, the leader sees it the other way around: employees have not yet given enough effort to warrant their (perceived) high expectations and demands.

When staff start expressing their desire for more and frustration that it's not being delivered, the root cause is often a lack of appreciation. Appreciation in leadership is like exercise for the body: it needs to be done regularly, with varying effort, and in different contexts to keep people from getting bored and getting stuck on a plateau.

We will need to review and implement changes to our engagement plan in 'Touchpoints'. Appreciation is a critical aspect of the touchpoint cadence, and we may have been slipping here. The good news is that this state is responsive. This means that though people may feel disgruntled, they are still aligned to the vision and purpose of the business. They want to participate and still have the energy to contribute. This state is ripe for harnessing. That goodwill can be tapped if the appreciation aspect is handled well.

STATE 4: Considered

Result: Engagement

Research across the web is consistent: work engagement seems to be extremely low. The statistics vary from 11 per cent engaged to 33 per cent engaged [14], which means at least two-thirds of the people at work do not enjoy it and are only doing the bare minimum. It seems that few of us care about our work, organisations, and the people we work with.

---

14   J. Harter, 'Moneyball for business: Employee engagement meta', *Gallup News*, 31 May, 2016.

But in my work I have not found this to be true. There are plenty of motivated and hard-working employees. One of the key components for successful teams and organisations is that there is a sense of growth, challenge, and fun. When engagement starts to drop off, the key element missing is growth, found in the practices of implementing 'Touchpoints'. This is the tipping point. Get it wrong, and you slide towards entitlement. Get it right, and we tip the scales towards loyalty.

In his remarkable book *Drive* [15], Daniel Pink determines that there are three things that really cause engagement and focus at work. These are: autonomy, mastery, and purpose. If we have something meaningful to focus on and we are given the freedom to pursue our contribution to it, all while honing and developing skills and having a sense of progress, then engagement will be the result.

Growth occurs when the individual's skills need to develop in order to meet new challenges. In fast-developing businesses, the pace of the work keeps the growth state alive. In more established businesses, where there is a clear-cut line of progression, establishing opportunities for growth can be more challenging. We tend to equate promotion with growth. However, with well-managed Touchpoints and effective leadership conversations (as described in the Talk chapter), we can deflect some of the frustration that might arise when promotions are limited. If individuals feel that they are stretching their thinking and ability, this is often as rewarding as a title and responsibility change.

STATE 5: Boundless

Result: Loyalty

This is the holy grail of any business. This is when we show up to work, excited for the day, and enjoy the work and the people we work with. We have a strong sense of commitment to the organisation and its purpose, and we feel proud of where we work. We have a sense that anything and everything is possible with the team we work with.

---

15   D. Pink, *Drive – The surprising truth about what motivates us*, New York, Riverhead Books, 2009.

We feel boundless. There is no doubt that each of us is committed to the long haul, to finding a way through, to doing our best, to putting in the hard yards and long hours if necessary.

Loyalty can also blind us to the failings of our peers and the system as a whole. If we place loyalty above other values, we can compromise our integrity. Think of Doug Stamper in *House of Cards*. Doug's one key value is loyalty. He will do anything for his boss Frank Underwood, including committing fraud, bullying, accepting blame for a murder he did not commit, and even committing a murder of his own. This is loyalty gone wrong. This kind of loyalty is based on the fear of losing power and position, not love.

Healthy loyalty creates engaged employees. This happens when individuals feel part of the system and appreciate the system, but do not owe their identity to it.

Healthy loyalty is generated from the structures that we have in place which facilitate appreciation, growth, and belonging. The more we can create a sense of belonging, the stronger the healthy loyalty is. These are the tools and strategies of developing a sense of 'Tribe'. To avoid the dangers of blind loyalty, your job as a leader at this stage is also to foster independent thinking and an open forum where people can challenge each other's ideas constructively. These are the skills of 'Talk'. In other words, we're building leaders and a system that supports them.

Building a systematic approach to engagement and loyalty helps us and our team adapt to changing cultural tides. We don't need to be taken by the current! We can steer our boat safely through workplace challenges. With our team, we can experience being boundless. This is where we achieve more and struggle less, where we feel inspired and focused, and where we belong.

Let's assess where you and your team currently sit on the Loyalty Ladder. Here are some reflection questions to help you gauge what is going on.

1. How many conversations have you had with team members about their level of satisfaction with their work? With their pay? With their professional development?

2. What kinds of comments do you hear when it comes to work satisfaction or workplace challenges?

3. Do you know your **employee** net promote score? This is a score out of 10 on how likely a staff member is to recommend your workplace as a good place to work.

4. Do you know your **manager** net promoter score? Again, this is asking your staff how likely they are to recommend you as someone good to work for.

5. Where does your team sit as a whole on the Loyalty Ladder?

6. Where do you think individuals sit on the Loyalty Ladder, including you?

Part 1

Tribe

How to build a team identity

Community is essential to our sense of safety. Ever since we crawled out of the mud and gathered in caves, we have sought the company of others. There was safety in numbers. In integral leadership theory, developing the capacity to belong and engage with a tribe is a core part of our development, and one of the earlier stages of leadership maturity [16]. Following the rules is what we are taught to do as children so that we interact safely and confidently with one another. Fitting in and belonging give us a huge sense of security and a safe way to engage with the world.

Fitting in and belonging are also biochemical needs. The hormone of trust is released in tightly formed teams and communities. When we feel safe, when we trust the people we are with, the lovely happy hormone of oxytocin is released [17].

Being part of a tribe also helps strengthen the immune system by reducing the impact of the stress hormone cortisol, and by promoting better sleep [18]. It simply feels good to be part of a group of people who like and trust each other. A group to belong to is a defence against the infections of loneliness and purposelessness. A tribe gives us a safe haven, a place to recharge, to feel nurtured, a home base.

The modern workplace has the potential to be our modern tribe. A sense of tribe, and the leadership gold of trust and oxytocin that comes with it, does not occur by default simply because you have people gathering in an office. It requires particular focus and attention to create the conditions that foster the flow of oxytocin.

---

16 B. Torbert and associates, *Action Inquiry: The Secret of Timely and Transforming Leadership*, San Francisco, Berrett-Koehler Publishers Inc., 2004.

17 There are some great resources on exploring the happy chemicals dopamine, endorphins, serotonin, and oxytocin. One of my favourites is by L.G. Breuning, *Habits of a Happy Brain: Retrain Your Brain To Boost Your Serotonin, Dopamine, Oxytocin & Endorphin levels*, Avon, Massachusetts, Adams Media, 2016.

18 There are a lot of great resources on this. See NaturalNews.com for a good overview of oxytocin.

What creates a sense of Tribe?

A Tribe has three important elements:

1. A **Team Compass** that makes explicit the purpose, shared values, and agreed behaviours of that group.

2. A **Team Flag** or a collection of flags that make the tribe identity visible and obvious to each other as well as to others.

3. A **Leadership Contract** that explicitly states the role of each person, in particular the role of the leader as steward of the tribe.

1. Team Compass

Without a core identity of being part something with a meaningful purpose, there is no sense of long-lasting pride. We can be proud of where we are from, of our parents, of our heritage, and of our achievements, but these are external markers of pride. To have a self-sustaining and durable sense of pride requires connection and alignment with meaningful purpose. No meaningful purpose, no loyalty.

Simon Sinek has grown famous around the globe for his work in *Start Your Why*[19]. In this book, he asserts that having something to believe in creates the conditions for committed followership and a happy sense of purpose. I believe that there are also additional factors that go towards creating lasting loyalty in a sense of tribe. These are the elements that form the points of a Team Compass. Like a real compass, they note the right direction. This helps you to make your way through the densest jungle of difficult situations or steer a path through the fog of the unknown, one step at a time, without going over the cliff of irrelevance.

---

19 S. Sinek, *Start With Why: How Great Leaders Inspire Others To Take Action*, London, Penguin Group, 2009.

The Team Compass points are:

- Values (what you care about)
- Purpose (who you serve)
- Qualities (how you behave)
- Results (what you do for the people you serve)

These form the core of your brand and can keep you navigating safely with what is most important.

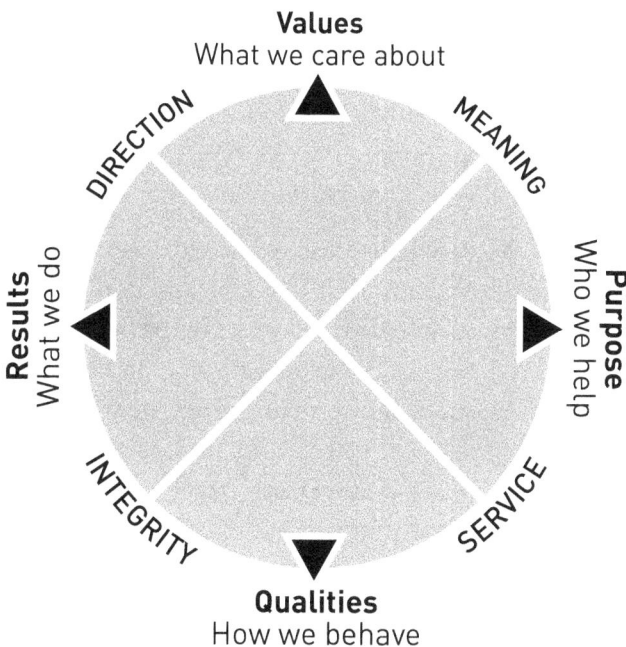

The RedBalloon example

RedBalloon is an Aussie business success story. It started as an online gift shop that provided experiences to customers rather than physical products. It is now one brand (or marketplace) sitting within a larger group, the Big Red Group. Their expansion has been due in part to their commitment to a great staff experience.

When I first became interested in corporate culture, on my podcast[20] I asked Megan Bromley, then head of Employee Experience at RedBalloon, to share her insights and strategies that helped build a culture that was named as one of the top 50 'Best Place to Work' by BRW award five years in a row (2009-2013). The organisation itself created a culture that is top-down from the implementation of values in action, and bottom-up for the custodianship and ongoing development of its culture.

I asked Megan to describe the culture of RedBalloon, and this is how she responded:

"I asked around and then created a word cloud. Some of the words were 'forward-thinking, ever-changing, pretty encouraging, happy, inspiring, awesome, exciting, rewarding'. That's just probably a snapshot. These things would have come from people that have worked at Red Balloon anywhere from six months up to five years."

At the heart of the RedBalloon business were the values. These values were distilled from the stories in the company itself: stories about when the company was founded, and why. Online they had a timeline of significant events in the company's history, and original stories that shaped the values of the company. They were brought to life with practices like the monthly RedBalloon 'Oscars'. This was a peer-to-peer recognition process where team members could nominate a colleague who demonstrated living their values. All nominations were shared with the team members, and in this way, stories continued to bring their values to life.

Each month, a winner was chosen from amongst the nominees and granted a reward from their 'Dreamcatcher'. The Dreamcatcher was a list of experiences that each individual created that was meaningful to them. Reward and recognition was thus curated for each individual, and personalised according to the individual's preferences, be it private or public. The Oscars were celebrated company-wide every year for a larger reward.

---

20   Z. Routh, 'Corporate culture: Megan Bromley Red Balloon Australia', audio blog post, Zoë Routh Leadership Podcast, 2016.

RedBalloon advocated the concept of Recognise Every Day (RED). They had a stockpile of cards that staff could grab and leave a thank you or appreciation note for a colleague. They had a public place where they listed 'Favourites', a preferred beverage or treat. If a team member wanted to recognise or appreciate a colleague, they checked the Favourites and could get them a special Lindt hot chocolate with a handwritten note to say that they were appreciated.

Management monitored employee engagement with the Employee Net Promoter Score[21]: "How likely are you to recommend this workplace to others?" This was done at least annually. The net promoter score was also used to evaluate the effectiveness of managers with the question: "How likely are you to recommend this person as someone to work for?"

Frequent short pulse checks were used to get timely, on-the-spot feedback at the end of a training cycle or after an event. There were usually no more than two questions, so it made it very easy for staff to respond.

At RedBalloon, Megan developed the Six Pillars of Employee Experience, which started on the first day of a new employee.

1. *Welcome:* Make sure that the induction for the new employee is well planned and prepared for their arrival. This includes things like a sign on front door, a buddy to show them around, and a meeting with head of employee experience.

2. *Flow:* Ensure that the new employee is made aware of the flow of communication and that they understand the what, how, and why of delivering on the RedBalloon purpose. This is cascaded through a regular cadence of meetings of various team levels.

3. *Tools:* Ensure that employees have the right tools and space to do their jobs. The feel of the office is important. Multiple work

---

21   This is a handy resource for understanding the Net Promoter Score and its application in many different contexts: F. Reichheld, *The Ultimate Question 2.0 – How Net Promoter Companies thrive in a customer-driven world*, Boston, Harvard Business School Publishing, 2011.

areas for different kinds of work help people to be productive, from customer service to project development.

4. *Grow:* Development is measured, challenged, and stretched. RedBalloon worked with profile instruments like HBDI [22] to create custom development plans.

5. *Appreciate:* Reward and recognition that is personalised, from the little things to the big things. These range from free experiences to company-wide celebrations.

6. *Wellness:* This includes a community happiness program, mentoring, a balance of the inside and outside aspects of work, and the quality of work (not just the hours worked).

RedBalloon had a very sophisticated and well-developed Team Compass that was integrated across their service delivery. They reaped the rewards with public recognition and a thriving business that has expanded rapidly.

---

22 http://www.herrmann.com.au/

With your team, spend some time exploring these questions to form your own Team Compass.

North

Values (what we care about)

1. What are the top three things we care about the most?

2. What is the biggest problem in the world?

3. What is the antidote to this problem?

4. Things we care about when it comes to: the world? People? Animals? Planet?

5. If we prioritised them, what would be the order?

East

Purpose (who we serve)

1. Who are the clients?

2. Who are the stakeholders?

3. Who are the beneficiaries of our work?

South

Qualities (how we behave)

1. How do we want to be known?

2. What are the behaviours we **don't** want?

3. What are the behaviours we **do** want?

West

Results (what we do for the people we serve)

1. What results do our clients achieve as a result of working with us?

2. What are the problems we solve for them?

3. What are the chief benefits they receive in working with us?

4. What do our clients say is the biggest benefit?

2. Team Flags

Team Flags brand us as a cohesive whole, to reinforce our values and identity for ourselves and for others. They bring to life what we create with our Team Compass.

'Flying the flag' means to show your support. Countries each have a flag to identify them as unique and as a symbol around which to unite. In organisations, we can create that sense of belonging, of identity, through tangible and visible symbols. Tribe pride is then reinforced through visible flags of tribal identity. So how can we address this in a corporate setting?

How to create an environment where people feel like they belong

Choose a team name

It's amazing how quickly people identify with a group. This happens even more quickly when the team creates a team name. Twitter staff call themselves Tweeps, at Yahoo everyone is a 'yahoo', Amazon staff are Amazonians and Microsoft people call themselves Microsofties. Even pragmatic team names help forge a bond: the Operations Team, the Marketing crew, and so on. Even if you disagree on many things, at least you can agree on your team name!

Take team photos

A business is only as good as its people. One way to demonstrate that they are important is to capture the team via a photo. This can get published on your website, on your internal communications platform, or printed old-school, framed and put in the relevant office space. If teams are more fluid, then you could do an annual or bi-annual photo. Or at staff events. Recording the people who bring the business to life is as important as recording the results of the business. No people, no results.

Create a team talisman

What do the Order of Australia, Rotary, and the US Navy SEALS all have in common? Their insignia is worn as a lapel pin that identifies the wearer as part of a group or experience. At Outward Bound, the lapel pin was a Blue Peter, a replica of the flag that was flown by ships that were leaving port 'outward bound'. It was given to participants who had completed the Challenge Course, a flagship outdoor program that spanned three weeks of arduous wilderness experiences.

Talismans can be wearables like bracelets, wristbands, tie pins, t-shirts, or jackets. They can be physical objects like mugs, mouse pads, business cards, rubber stress toys, and pens. They can also showcase iconic objects. One of my favourite examples is at Mindvalley, an online personal development platform. They have a life-size figure of Wonder Woman in their office[23]. Part of their induction process involves swearing to uphold the principles and values of Mindvalley, while holding on to a statuette of Wonder Woman, their emblem of courage and awesomeness!

Showcase
Creating tribes with the Fearless Bustards

On all of the outdoor experiential programs I lead, I ask the groups to choose a name that best represents their values as a collective. This is a way of finding out what is most important to the group (as per the Team Compass) and building a common sense of purpose.

One of my Mastermind groups struggled for the first few days of their expedition to settle on a name. I think I was more frustrated than they were, and sensing my frustration, they dragged out the decision-making for fun. They suggested ridiculous names like 'Lemmings' – all following blindly – and eventually settled on 'Fearless Bustards'. This occurred as they spotted a bustard (a type of bird). I objected because I thought they said 'bastards', not having any knowledge of bustards at the time. So Fearless Bustards they became, and still refer to one another as such.

---

23   Check it out at Mindvalley: https://blog.mindvalley.com/how-mindvalley-evolved/

Implement

1. Brainstorm a name for your work team or group. Anything will do, as long as everyone agrees to adopt it.

2. Take a team photo at a particular celebration point, like the beginning of the year, end of year, or quarterly retreat. Hang it somewhere where everyone can see it. Consider a wall or hallway for team or organisation photos.

3. Explore what kind of talisman you could adopt. Some ideas are: bracelets, wrist bands, phone covers, stickers, satchel bags, mouse pads, mugs, beanies, scarves. Pick up the corporate gift catalogue and see what it inspires.

3. Leadership Contract

Developing an identity is the fun aspect of developing a tribe. There is, however, a more serious aspect to it. We saw from the first section that there are legal requirements and obligations for employees when it comes to loyalty. To develop genuine loyalty, there are leadership commitments that leaders need to undertake to foster loyalty and belonging.

In this age of collaboration, with its agile approach to fast prototyping and working in matrix organisations, conventional expectations of leadership have changed. A leader's unofficial commitments form a leadership contract. This is one where the employer and leader provide certain functions to ensure a more engaging workplace.

In the past, leaders were tasked with looking out for the safety of the tribe. They were the defenders of the realm who fought battles to protect the turf and its members. They were often the biggest, strongest, and shrewdest people in the group. In exchange they received certain privileges, such as the best food, the choice of mate, or best accommodation. In contemporary terms, this has come to mean the best office, the best parking spot, and so on.

There is now a move towards flattening these kinds of privileges for more egalitarian access to resources. For some privileges, there are still particular responsibilities. These privileges that are granted in exchange for leadership responsibilities may include increased pay, access to private information and decision-making processes, or more annual leave.

There is a large range of main responsibilities that leaders need to embrace in their Leadership Contract with their teams:

Protection

From others: They may not need to throttle a raging Pterodactyl, but the leader's role as protector of the team is still critical. Protection includes things like representing the team or organisation's interests to external stakeholders, customers, or suppliers. This includes negotiating on the team's behalf. Sometimes it also includes backing the team and its members in the face of unfair criticism of its performance. The leader must back their team. They also need to protect the team from overwork or overloading. The leader should intimately know the team's capabilities and be able to broker appropriate work assignments on their behalf. This does not mean that the team doesn't get stretched or challenged!

From each other and themselves: The leader needs to be mindful of how internal dynamics can go pear-shaped, quickly. The leader needs to foster a spirit of collaboration and healthy constructive dialogue. They need to make that sure every voice is heard and every idea is assessed. The leader also needs to think critically about the team's performance and engagement, and not be lulled into a false sense of satisfaction due to happy camaraderie. This is how blind spots develop. Sometimes tensions arrive under pressure; the team leader needs to know the individuals, what the survival triggers are, and how to defuse these when they arrive.

Direction

Coordinating activities is still an important aspect of the Team Leadership Contract. In a matrix organisation or on multiple project teams, it's important to know how to and who makes decisions. Having clear criteria for what gets accepted, rejected, and why helps prevent negative reactions.

Delegating duties and explaining why each person has these responsibilities keeps people from catastrophising. There is less room for imagining that there are favourites. Likewise, if we need to name a deputy to stand in, in case of absences or emergencies, it's important to explain why the person chosen fits the bill. Otherwise people can feel left out or ostracised or jealous. When these reasons are transparent, people may not always agree or approve of the decisions, but at least they feel that they are respected enough to be told why.

Focus

The leader acts as the steward for the Team Compass. They keep team members on track and clarify the nature of their purpose, their individual roles, how these fit in to the bigger picture, and what goals are meaningful, clear, and purposeful.

Feel

Morale and the vibe of the group is also steered and monitored by the leader. This is done by celebrating wins, having frequent positive experiences, and getting to know each other as people. Accountability is a priority, and progress is made visible. When people know what is expected of them and they can see how their contribution makes a difference, they feel more engaged.

Framework

This is an expansion of the Team Compass. It includes ground rules for engagement and meetings, and outlines what is acceptable or not when the team comes together in meetings or on projects. It also includes a documented process for resolving issues and giving and receiving feedback. One of the most fundamental rituals for any team, which is instigated by the leader to make it a safe experience for all, is to review and learn from failures. Relationship to failure is important for healthy experimentation and progress.

Take the Team Leadership Contract Assessment and see where you can fill in the gaps in your leadership. Tick off all that apply below:

Protection

- ☐ I represent my team interests to external stakeholders: customers and suppliers.
- ☐ I back my team in the case of undue, unfair, or unbalanced criticism of role, function, and performance.
- ☐ I manage up.
- ☐ I promote innovation/ideas/suggestions/perspectives to ensure we cycle ideas.
- ☐ I review and address blind spots.
- ☐ I manage tension between colleagues.
- ☐ I am mindful of and manage potential amygdala hijack triggers.

Direction

- ☐ My team and I are clear about decisions: what gets accepted, what gets rejected, and why.
- ☐ My team and I are clear about delegation: who does what and why.
- ☐ My team and I are clear about deputation: who steps in for the leader and why.

Focus

- ☐ My team and I are clear about purpose, the 'why' of the team and its various projects.
- ☐ We have clear goals that excite and inspire us.
- ☐ My team and I are clear about the role each team member must play, relative to the accomplishment of the goals.

- [ ] We are clear on our roles and these are documented clearly.

- [ ] My team and I are clear about the relationship each team member has to the rest of the team members, and how they support or guide each other and the project.

Feel

- [ ] My team and I celebrate the wins and achievements of individuals and the team as a whole.

- [ ] My team and I have repeated positive experiences and feel close to one another.

- [ ] We get to know each other as people, sharing our background and aspects of our personal world.

- [ ] We have unique rituals that are part of our team's culture.

- [ ] We have frequent social experiences.

- [ ] We make progress visible and this is how we stay accountable.

- [ ] We manage projects with short timeframes through accountability and effective, regular feedback.

- [ ] We manage projects with longer timeframes though good structure, process, and motivation.

- [ ] I set the mood deliberately with my own.

Framework

- [ ] We have ground rules for how the team is to engage with each other, and this includes acceptable and unacceptable behaviour.

- [ ] We have a clear framework and guidelines for how feedback is delivered, and expectations on how it is to be received and processed, both individually and as a team.

- [ ] We have a clear and documented process for handling disagreements at an individual and team level.

- [ ] We regularly celebrate as well as learn from failures.

Part 2

Touchpoints

How to build meaningful interactions to build loyalty

Identity and team cohesion requires more than just a Team Compass, flags, and intention of a leadership contract. It needs dedicated practice and a regular pattern of positive interactions.

For many new managers, a common and painful discovery is how difficult it is to do the 'people' side of the job. Many bemoan the loss of actually doing the technical aspects of their previous role, as they find themselves face-to-face with a new set of skills to be learned: engaging with people.

How we interact with the people we support has a massive impact on employee experience, and their sense of engagement and loyalty. Gallup found that employers who boost their engagement results focus on management development programs instead of just employee engagement measurements. Fewer than 10 per cent of leaders are naturally suited to managerial roles, while others can be coached and developed into the skills[24]. Think about your own experience with a supervisor. How often did you speak with them? How rewarding were the interactions? How did you feel during and after? Were you uplifted and energised? Or deflated and confused?

In my time as an employee, what I remember is not the specifics of the work, but how I felt before and after an engagement with my boss. I suspect it's paternalistic in nature: the desire for approval and recognition that echoes some sort of parent-child relationship. Simon Sinek latches onto family dynamics in *Leaders Eat Last*. He says, "Every single employee is someone's son or daughter. Like a parent, a leader of a company is responsible for their precious lives."[25] While I appreciate the sentiment of grave responsibility that a leader has for those in their care, I also see a successful workplace experience

---

24   L. Emond, '2 reasons why employee engagement programs fall short', Gallup News, 15 August 2017.

25   S. Sinek, *Leaders Eat Last – Why some teams pull together and others don't*, London, Portfolio Penguin, 2014.

as co-creative. The other party has to come to the party! In the meantime, as leaders we can create the experiences that draw others into wanting to come to the party in the first place.

In Part 2: Touchpoints we explore the practical aspects of experiences: the why, when, where, how, and how often of interacting with team members. This includes:

A. **The Five Currencies of Employee Engagement**. An examination of the drivers at work and how to customise rewards and recognition plans.

B. **The Touchpoint Cadence**. This lays out a daily to yearly frequency of different types of engagements that you can undertake.

C. **The Team Engagement Wheel**. A deeper dive into a daily or weekly interaction cycle to set intentions and establish positive focus.

D. **Common Ground**. Getting to know your people, as people.

A. The Five Currencies of Employee Engagement

There are different types of currencies that individuals value. These are:

1. Survival needs: Represented by money

2. Belonging: A sense of community and identity

3. Appreciation: Development of esteem through personal, individualised acknowledgment

4. Status: Recognition that delivers a sense of prestige

5. Growth: A sense of progress and development.

1. Survival needs

How much money is enough? What is fair pay? As it is such a complex field, it is legislated, and details can be found at the Fair Pay

Ombudsman website [26] including allowances, penalty rates, and base pay rates. The underlying issue is far subtler. How much pay does an employee feel they *deserve*? This is a subjective matter and is coloured by the following factors:

· Past experience or salary threshold. "If I once earned that, I become accustomed to that level. If I get paid less, it feels like a downgrade and I am not being paid my worth."

· What others are getting paid. "Am I getting paid fairly in comparison?"

· What I aspire to earn. "Does my current income match what I think I am capable of?"

Money is never the first reason people leave, but it's often the first excuse. People will tolerate a smaller wage if the other currencies are fabulous. If one or more of the currencies are sub-par, money becomes the nudge that people need to seek work elsewhere.

2. Belonging

As in Part 1: Tribe, a place to belong and an identity or group shape a sense of security. It boosts our sense of pride and increases serotonin as a result (another feel-good hormone). This is not about creating a homogenous group where everyone is a clone. Diversity of all kinds is essential: age, race, religion, background, perspective. Unity around values and purpose, however, is essential. This is what creates true belonging.

3. Appreciation

In their fabulous book *The 5 Languages of Appreciation in the Workplace: Empowering organisations by encouraging people* [27], Gary Chapman and Paul White state, "Why is feeling appreciated so important in a work setting? Because each of us wants to know what we are doing matters."

---

26   See www.fairwork.gov.au

27   G.D. Chapman and P. White, *The 5 Languages of Appreciation in the Workplace: Empowering Organisations by Encouraging People*, Chicago, Northfields Publishing, 2011.

Chapman and White's 5 Languages of Appreciation in the Workplace include:

1. Words of Affirmation: Praise for accomplishments, personality, or character traits

2. Quality Time: Giving focused attention

3. Acts of Service: When others reach out to help

4. Tangible Gifts: Valued by the recipient, not just the giver

5. Physical Touch: Handshake, high five, hand on the shoulder, a hug.

One size does not fit all. Depending on cultural preferences or personal space, a leader needs to know what their team members prefer (in terms of appreciation) and shift their approach to match. Likewise, it's also helpful if team members know each other's respective preferences, to encourage appreciation in the mode that is most, well, appreciated!

4. Status

When I am delivering leadership conversation workshops, I often cite David Rock's work[28] on contemporary threats in the workplace that cause a fight or flight response, or an 'amygdala hijack'. These include status, uncertainty, lack of autonomy, relatedness (knowing who is a friend or foe), and fairness. In my workshops I get nods to all the triggers, except status. Here people tend to harrumph and deny that this is a threat for them, commenting that status doesn't mean that much to them.

Oh, *really?!*

I challenge them to think about a time when their work was denigrated, their opinion disregarded, or their expertise not taken in to account. That's when they sit up and exclaim, "You're right! That drives me crazy!"

---

28 D. Rock, *Your Brain At Work: Strategies for overcoming distraction, regaining focus, and working smarter all day long*, Pymble, Australia, HarperCollins, 2009.

Recognition of our status comes hand-in-hand with earlier stages of leadership maturity, when we are first establishing ourselves in our careers and developing our expertise. Status is not just about the symbols such as the title, the workplace space, or the parking space. These are the things that people dismiss initially as inconsequential, until these symbols are removed. Like it or not, we associate our place in the tribe – therefore our sense of security and safety – with these flags of status. Remove them and we feel threatened. At work this looks like frustration, anger, disappointment, or even insubordination. Pecking order is a metaphor for humans and not just chicken behaviour, because it has a real impact in our social rules. Status symbols are a way of maintaining the pecking order, and often the group harmony as a result. Be mindful of how you allocate and change status symbols. They are anything but superficial to the recipients.

Status is also about recognition of a job well done and acknowledgment of a performance that met or exceeded expectations. The kind of singling out, whether done privately or publicly, reinforces our sense of self. When others seek our opinion, it reinforces our sense of worth and having something of value to contribute.

5. Growth

Development has been on the work radar ever since Maslow listed his Hierarchy of Needs from those of basic survival to self-actualisation. We are wired to grow and progress. Even nature has life-force encoded with growth.

In *Drive* [29], Dan Pink determines that along with purpose, mastery and autonomy are also needed for employee engagement. This helps leaders design tasks and responsibilities where people can excel, in roles that are neither too overwhelming nor too restrictive. The balance needs to be just right: enough challenge to stretch but not to overwhelm, and enough autonomy to feel independent but not lost in the wilderness.

---

29   D. Pink, *Drive – The surprising truth about what motivates us*, Edinburgh, Canongate, 2009.

In *The Game Changer*[30], Dr Jason Fox explains that the most important way to create motivation for work is to "make progress visible". A sense of meaningful progress, of developing and learning, is integral to bringing meaning to our work. Otherwise we are just cogs spinning endlessly for vacuous rewards.

We need to ensure that work is meaningful, that people are learning and growing in their work, and that progress is visible. This is the 'gamification' component of Jason's work. Gamification is applying game design to the work context. In games we keep score, and there are levels to indicate progress. A simple progress bar, pie chart, or graph that reveals the distance to goal and completion of work towards that goal gives us the dopamine hit that lights up the motivation centre.

What about perks, though? Are these what matters most to employees? Many experiments have been undertaken to explore what will encourage employee engagement and loyalty. According to Michelle Checketts in her article 'Why Perks Don't Result in Employee Engagement'[31], she explores the competitive Silicon Valley environment. She says:

"Companies have engaged in a 'perks arms race' by offering to take care of your daily life needs:

· Google will feed you all your meals, do your laundry, and even run your errands via Google Shopping Express.

· Beyond food, Twitter will also valet park your car when you arrive at the office, provide a Caltrain pass, or give you the option to meet at a designated company shuttle stop.

· Facebook is building a 394-unit apartment complex located two miles from its headquarters, which will feature a gym, pool, pet spa, coffee shop, sports bar, and more.

---

30   J. Fox, *The Game Changer: How to use the science of motivation with the power go game design to shift behaviour, shape culture, and make clever happen*, Milton, Wiley & Sons, 2014.

31   M. Checketts, 'Why Perks Don't Result in Employee Engagement', *DecisionWise* (accessed 23rd January 2018).

Perks alone are not enough to result in employee engagement. They can keep employees satisfied, but they can't engage hearts, hands, and minds to give discretionary effort."

So while our staff may brag about perks, they won't stay for them. Perks are nice, but growth, impact, and meaning matter more.

Showcase
The five currencies in tree planting

One spring during my university days, I worked as a tree planter for a company called Bugbusters. Tree planting was an arduous and lucrative way for students to make money over spring and summer. We were paid per tree seedling planted, usually between 10 and 25 cents per tree, and could earn upwards of $200 per day, a veritable fortune in those days. In one spring season I could earn enough to cover my tuition fees and some of my living expenses for the year.

The work was back-breaking. Armed with a shovel and saddlebags laden with hundreds of tree seedlings, we trudged over the wreckage left from logging and dug little holes to plug the seedlings into. Scurry like a goat, scratch away surface debris with the shovel, plunge the shovel into the soil, bend over, place a seedling into the newly created slot, then seal with an aggressive heel kick. Repeat, literally thousands of times per day.

If we look at the Five Currencies of Employee Engagement, we had a few:

The money was good. We belonged to a fun-loving business – how could you not be with a name like Bugbusters? Status was conveyed through results: the more you planted, the more high fives and admiration you received. A 'highballer' was someone who consistently out-planted everyone else. It was seriously competitive.

As a tree planter, it was easy to feel the sense of progress. I started the day with a fresh patch of terrain marked out by chosen landmarks, and I planted trees until that block was full. The empty tree containers grew as we bagged out (emptied the saddlebags of tree seedlings) and then bagged up again from the tree supply boxes. Empty boxes meant trees in the ground and money in the pocket.

So what was missing?

Appreciation. The money, adventure, and progress could only take us so far. As the work was unrelenting, morale started to deteriorate, and the happy applause from our foreman (called 'Venus') was lacklustre.

So with my friends Jo and Gary, we staged an intervention and suggested we have 'Christmas' on our next day off. We pulled names out of a hat and had to create something for that person. No store-bought things, just what we could make. Purchasing of supplies was allowed. When the big day arrived, we were blown away. People had really made an effort to produce something for their peer. Even Venus was relaxed and smiling! It really shifted the mood and attitude in the group.

These shared experiences are a welcome break in the pattern of work. They give us something to look forward to and focus our creative energy on. With our newfound sense of camaraderie, we renamed ourselves the Love Crew. These experiences also create bonds that last. Jo ended up marrying Venus a few years later and settling in western Canada, where members of the Love Crew still gather.

Assess your strengths and challenges against the five currencies:

1. How well does work meet your own financial survival needs? Are you satisfied or dissatisfied? What about those in your team and workplace? How is compensation seen and experienced?

2. How much do you feel that you belong to something important? How robust is the sense of community in your workplace?

3. What are your own appreciation preferences? What about those of your team? How do you incorporate these in your day-to-day practices?

4. Do you feel recognised in your work? What status symbols do you enjoy? What about others? How do you recognise other people's performance?

5. How are you growing and developing at work? What are you currently learning? What have you learned over these past 12 months? What is your current development plan? What is the development plan for those on your team?

B. The Touchpoint Cadence model

Creating a meaningful employee engagement plan

The Touchpoint Cadence model is a way to design an engagement plan that builds goodwill and loyalty. There are three areas we need to always be mindful of: **People**, **Process**, and **Progress**. How we approach each of these changes depends on the timing, be it daily, weekly, quarterly, or yearly.

TOUCHPOINT CADENCE

	Daily	Weekly/ Monthly	Quarterly	Yearly
	Momentum	*Increment*	*Calibration*	*Leverage*
People	Care	Acknowledge	Recognition	Reward
Process	Clarify	Smooth	Review	Design
Progress	Check	View	Re-Set	Celebrate
Experiences	**Presence**	**Pause**	**Punctuation**	**Peak**

Daily and weekly touchpoints

The purpose of daily touchpoints is to build momentum in the relationship with the leader and members of the team. These touchpoints can be implemented one-to-one or in a team. Sharing our presence is what the team experiences. In daily touchpoints, we want to show people that we care, clarify any issues or challenges they may have, and check on progress against goals/projects/objectives.

In the weekly meeting, we then want to make incremental progress. What people experience is pressing 'pause' on their activity to catch their breath, review what is working or not, and make corrections. Our **People** focus is to acknowledge contributions in the process and results, and to take a pulse check. We could get people to give a one-word summary about how they feel about the week, team, or project, give a thumbs up or down rating on the same, or a rating out of ten. It's also a good time to acknowledge workloads, deadlines, and share any wins or personal challenges.

The **Process** focus for the weekly touchpoint is to ask: what systems need tweaking? Is there any duplication? What else might be standing in the way of getting the job done? A weekly review of **Progress** is incredibly motivating. If we have a progress bar or milestone marker, now is the time to update it. Savour the sense of satisfaction that comes from moving a progress indicator forward!

What this looks like in practice:

Timing: It depends on the flow of work practices. Mondays work well for setting up the week. Fridays work well for reviewing the week and getting ready for the following one.

Duration: No more than 30 minutes.

Agenda:

- **People:** Round robin (one person at a time) of individual wins, challenges, or weekly deadlines.

- **Process:** Roadblock removal to ask: what needs clarifying? What needs streamlining? Come with questions or solutions.

- **Progress:** Review the dashboard/activity road map of your choice to mark progress for the week. Celebrate milestones.

- **Finish:** Thumbs up or down on enthusiasm for the week, or rating of 1-10 on morale. Follow up with individuals if there is negative feedback.

Amp It Up: Add food! Since the days of old, we have developed social bonds through sharing meals. We can add food as part of the meetings. People can contribute by creating a roster of who brings a snack. Each person gets a turn at honouring the tribe and their place in it through their culinary delights. The food always comes after the agenda – to provide an incentive to get through it and not get distracted with "Can you please pass the biscuits?"

Some other successful touchpoints include:

- A multicultural lunch where people bring a dish from their respective heritage
- Melbourne Cup Day lunch where everyone brings a plate
- Valentine's Day cards and chocolates. This can be like a Secret Santa format (pull a name out of the hat)
- Just go out for a meal. This is always delightful treat.

Quarterly touchpoints

In *The New Rules of Management*[32], Peter Cook suggests 90 days as a good block of time for project implementation. It's a reasonable period to generate results on experiments and to see progress against bigger goals. When we have a quarterly review, it gives us a chance to recalibrate our effort, and sometimes our expectations.

A quarterly touchpoint gives us enough time to collect data against our desired results. Thus we can recognise individual and team performers against their activity and performance. In the **People** area, we can review our engagement against the Team Compass. Are we living up to the values and behaviours we laid out? How would we rate our level of performance as a group? As individuals?

This is a good time to review **Process** from this perspective:

Is our work delivering on our most important priority? How is our problem-identification process? Do we have enough creative friction to get new ideas happening? What do we need to keep doing, stop doing, or start doing? Our progress focus at the quarterly touchpoint is to reset priorities, determine new 90-day projects, review lessons learned, and get re-energised for the next 90 days. They are a great punctuation point in a yearly calendar. It's a great time to get the team offsite. A change in scenery can lend gravitas to this ritual.

---

32   P. Cook, *The New Rules of Management: How to Revolutionise Productivity, Innovation, and Engagement by Implementing Projects That Matter*, Milton, John Wiley & Sons, 2013.

What this looks like in practice:

Timing: Again, this depends on your workflow peaks and troughs. You need to plan four of these per year. Think of them in themes like Momentum, Course Correction, Double Down, and Bring It Home.

Location: Offsite, preferably somewhere with a good view. Failing that, somewhere with great food.

Duration: Depending on the size and scope of your team, they can span from two hours to two days in length.

Agenda:

- **People:**
  - Recognition for results. Results are provided ahead of time from data collected against measurement strategies.[33]
  - Team Compass: what's working and what's not? Where can we excel?

- **Process** for discussion:
  - Is our work delivering on our most important priority? How can we tell?
  - What do we need to keep doing, stop doing, and start doing?
  - Creative thinking review[34] of our key project.

- **Progress** for discussion:
  - Over the last 90 days, what went well? Why? What are you most proud of? What did you learn?
  - For the next 90 days, what result should would we focus on? What project will help us deliver on that result? How will you stretch yourself over these next 90 days?

---

33 Do you and your business a favour and develop meaningful measures that will demonstrate whether your work is making an impact. The definitive source is Stacey Barr's work. See S. Barr, *Prove It – How to create a high-performance culture and measurable success*, Sydney, Wiley & Sons, 2017.

34 There are many excellent creative thinking tools and approaches. Start with Ken Hudson's book, *The Idea Generator – Tools for Growth*, Crows Nest, Allen & Unwin, 2007.

- Pre-emptive post-mortem: Imagine that the next 90 days are complete. What might have gotten in our way that would have caused us to fail? What could we do instead to prevent this failure?

Yearly touchpoints

Yearly touchpoints are celebrations! Every year we gather to discuss peak experiences that create a sense of team lore. These are significant gatherings that can leverage cultural goodwill throughout the year. This is when we give rewards, which are curated from people's individual preferences. Thoroughly analysing and airing the highs and lows of the year helps mark meaningful progress. It's also a good time to plan the next 12 months and design the experiences to come. In this way we keep leaping forward from our past experiences.

Yearly touchpoints are highlights. If we design them well, they can become defining moments for us, our team, and the business. Chip and Dan Heath published a great book on how to create these magic moments, called *The Power of Moments – Why Certain Experiences Have Extraordinary Impact* [35]. Their research shows that there are a few important things that we can do to make ordinary moments have an impact. These are:

- Elevation: Boost sensory pleasure and, if appropriate, a measure of surprise. Think big, bold, flavoursome, and special.

- Pride: Celebrate milestones, results, reaching targets, new promotions, acts of courage, and acts of generosity.

- Insight: Provide experiences that create deep insight around a difficult issue. This can be done with site visits, client guest speakers, case studies, or actual experiences.

- Connection: Bring people together for celebration. Staff parties of all sorts provide a great vehicle for this.

---

35   C. Heath and D Heath, The Power of Moments – Why Certain Experiences Have Extraordinary Impact, London, Bantam Press, 2017.

What this looks like in practice:

Timing: Again, this depends on workflow peaks and troughs. Choose a time that avoids peak periods or peak family demands, such as during school holidays. The yearly touchpoint needs a focus of mystique, of special investment (of time, energy or money).

Location: Offsite, preferably somewhere with a good view – think big! Some leaders go overseas: to a Balinese resort in the mountains or to an adventure resort in New Zealand. There are plenty of fantastic spots in Australia as well. One of my clients takes his team to a wilderness cabin in the Snowy Mountains for their team planning retreat.

Duration: Depending on the size and scope of your team, plan for one to three days in length.

Agenda:

- **People:**
    - Rewards must be personally meaningful for the individual, created just for them.
    - Be aware that employees may need to sacrifice time/home commitments to attend.
- **Process** To deliver as a group:
    - Theme word for the year
    - Results map and measures [36]
    - Key improvement projects and milestones to deliver these results.
- **Progress** This is all about celebrating! Share:
    - Highlights
    - Lowlights
    - Turning points
    - Moments of Truth
    - 'Kodak moment' – memories worth keeping.

---

36   S. Barr, *Prove It – How to create a high-performance culture and measurable success*, Sydney, Wiley & Sons, 2017.

Showcase
The case for staff awards

Awards can be serious (such as RedBalloon's nomination for someone who best demonstrated the organisation's values) or more playful. Sometimes you can give every person in a group a special award of their own, made up to commemorate a great (or not so great) moment.

I once handed out a cucumber for the Cucumber Award to a participant named Lou, for keeping cool as a cucumber in times of high stress. Except for that one time when, totally out of character, he dropped his bundle and slammed the car door in frustration. There were extenuating circumstances: it was on a challenging leadership program; it was 4am; the group had no idea where they were; they could not crack the clue; and the group's problem-solving ability was deteriorating and becoming dysfunctional. Lou, normally a highly respected and influential strategic thinker, was not coping well with the ambiguity. Actually, none of them were! It was a defining moment for each of them as individuals and as a whole.

Amplify yearly Touchpoints – outside!

When we are out of our usual surroundings in a stunning natural setting, we actually change our bio-chemistry. We boost the feel-good hormones of endorphins and our cortisol level drops. In an outdoor setting, stress melts and spirits lift. Together in the great outdoors, we can amplify yearly Touchpoints and team engagement with shared experiences. 'Out of the ordinary' events create a sense of lore.

Intensity builds memory circuits. The more intense an experience, the more elevated our emotions, so the more memorable the interaction. Novelty creates a sense of excitement and highlights the special nature of the experience. We also bond through adversity. Nature can be challenging! Cold, wet, and even hot weather can bring us back to elemental concerns of survival and looking after basic human needs. When we go through a difficult experience together, we see each other at our most vulnerable, and at our most courageous. Façades melt away, and we see each other as human beings.

The most remarkable organisations create the most remarkable experiences for their teams. You can include outdoor adventures as part of your engagement plan. Some ideas include:

· Lunchtime walks in a park

· Quarterly or yearly retreats in remote natural settings

· A travel adventure escape with a professional tour company

· Outdoor experiential programs designed to develop and hone team leadership and engagement skills.

Implement

Plan your daily touchpoint

· What questions can you use to check in with people? (See the next section on the Engagement Wheel)

· When and where works best for your team?

Plan your weekly or monthly touchpoint

· Choose the day and time for your weekly touchpoint

· Plan the standing agenda

· Launch!

Plan your quarterly touchpoint

· Determine the themes for each touchpoint

· Choose a location

· Craft an agenda

· Announce and book it in

· Gather the data for the review of results as you go

Plan your yearly touchpoint

· Choose the time of year

· Choose the location

· Consider how you might amplify the experience using the Heath brothers' suggestions, particularly sensory enhancement and surprise

· Gather information about your team members' appreciation preferences and how they prefer to be rewarded

· Prepare the agenda

· Announce and book it in!

C. Team Engagement Wheel

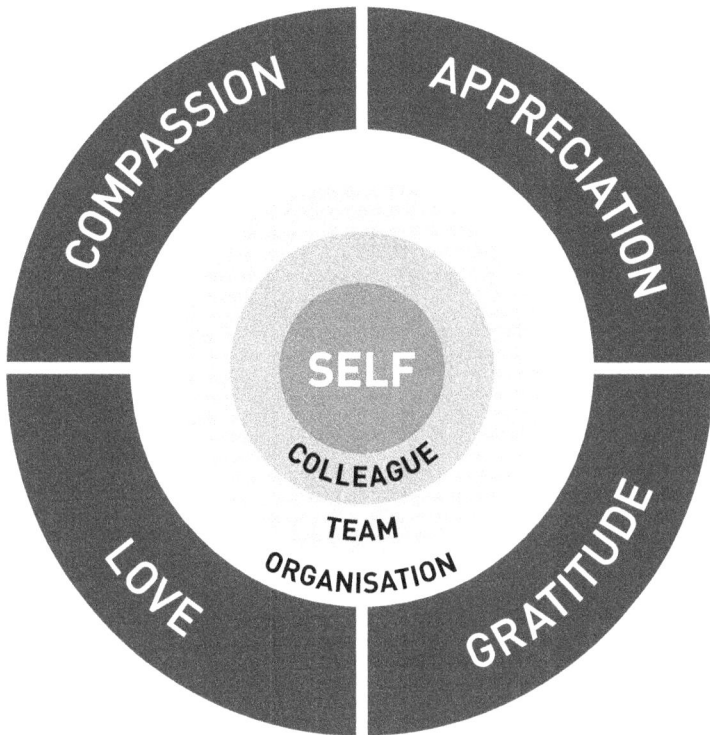

As leaders we need to focus on recognising the good stuff, as well as dealing with the tough stuff like criticism and constructive feedback. The Engagement Wheel is about putting the majority of our focus, day-to-day, on the positives. It is this that will lay the groundwork for success.

It's in the daily interactions where trust is carefully grown, one conversation at a time. These can be crafted and handled with care by using the Engagement Wheel. This is an expansion of the daily Touchpoints described in the previous section. I developed the Engagement Wheel by asking: "How do we start to shift attitudes and create the space where people feel welcome and safe at work? What can we do as leaders for ourselves, first and foremost, to set our own mood and intention?"

As a concept, the Engagement Wheel comes from the meditation practice designed to hone four 'attitudes'. The wheel cycles through four attitudes – **appreciation**, **gratitude**, **love**, and **compassion** – as it applies to individual and team engagement.

At a glance, start with the centre of the wheel and move outwards. Consider appreciation and apply it across the four different layers, starting with appreciation of self. We often fail to do this piece! It is appreciation of self, and what we're doing well. Next is appreciation of colleagues. What do you appreciate about their efforts, contribution or attitude? Then appreciation of team – ask what is the team doing well collectively? Finally, appreciation of organisation. What do we appreciate in being part of this company?

1. Start off well with appreciation

When you start the daily practice, ask yourself: "What can I appreciate about myself, my colleagues, or just one other colleague, my team, and my organisation?" When you do this practice, you start to feel good and experience a quiet sense of relief.

If you create a low threshold for happiness, by using the appreciation attitude, this will serve you better. The lowest threshold is, "I wake up breathing. It's a good start." You can express appreciation for yourself as a daily practice or incorporate this into your team meetings and encourage people to share what they appreciate.

2. The next attitude is gratitude

Sometimes it's not that easy to get into gratitude, especially if you are having a bad day. It's too big a gear to shift. It's like going from first gear to fifth: if you don't have enough revs happening, you're likely to stall.

So ask: "What am I grateful for, about myself, colleague, team, or organisation?" Another great question is, "Who can I thank?" It's incredibly powerful because it feels really good to thank somebody for something that they've done which you've benefited from.

3. Now, let's deal with the next higher-level attitude, which is love

It's a four-letter word that doesn't often appear in contemporary workplaces. When you love yourself at work, you show up with such a different kind of energy. When you love your colleagues, your team, and your organisation, that grows into passion, conviction, and determination. Love is one of the most useful emotions we can have in leadership.

Here's a starting sentence you could incorporate into your engagement practices. "I love what you did here." You can give feedback around this. "Susan. I love what you did with this particular project. I love how you engaged on this particular idea. I love how you ..." You can also try: "What I love about this team is... What I love about myself is…"

People might stumble a little on this last one. It sounds arrogant, until you say it with humility. You could say, "What I love about myself is that I'm continually trying to do my best. I may not always get it right, yet what I hold has something I value, and what I love about myself is that I will keep going." When we claim our strengths like that, it's incredibly powerful.

4. The fourth attitude is compassion

Compassion is an amplified version of love. It's important to make the distinction: from the lowest to the highest level of emotional states, we have sympathy, then empathy, then compassion.

Sympathy is: "I feel sorry for you. I see you're in pain, and I feel bad about that."

Empathy is: "I see you're in pain, and I can feel your pain."

Compassion is: "I can see and appreciate your pain, and if I can, I will assist you to do what you can to alleviate your pain." It's a proactive, constructive way of helping others deal with their pain.

We express compassion by starting with ourselves. The first way we do this is by not saying unkind things to ourselves. We frequently say, "Oh. I'm such an idiot," or, "I stuffed that up." We are very hard on ourselves. Start by showing some compassion for yourself. If you stuffed up it's okay, as long as you learn from it. Be compassionate in how you treat yourself with your mistakes. Don't linger in shame, guilt, and remorse. Learn from it. Make amends. Apologise. Move on. Apply what you've learned to new relationships. Showing compassion to yourself is really important.

Day-to-day with your team, you can ask the compassion question, "Who can I help today? How can I show compassion to my fellow colleagues?" It doesn't mean rescuing them, however. That's the danger: when we're compassionate, we just want to go in and save the day.

Compassion is more about expressing concern and support, and doing what you can to assist people to help themselves. It could be as simple as helping them move some tables and chairs in a meeting room. That's an act of compassion. "Hmm. I see you've got a job here. Let me help." Or, it could be, checking in on them. "I understand you've got a lot of big deadlines right now. You look a bit stressed. What's going on?"

Now, you imagine how you might feel at work if you used the Engagement Wheel on a daily basis. What if you practised appreciation, gratitude, love, and compassion as a part of everyday life with your team? Daily meditation practice using the Ishaya Bright Path meditation techniques has changed how I show up. I'm more centred, calm, and emotionally resilient than ever before. If we do this as a collective, this will magnify across our business experience.

Showcase
How meditation helped develop
The Engagement Wheel

I trained with the Bright Path[37]. It's a meditation practice that is agnostic and non-religious, and is based on thousands of years of meditation practice and tradition. The practitioners teach four

---

37   See www.thebrightpath.com

'attitudes', or techniques on how to slip into the process of meditation. This is so you can reap all the benefits of it, such as feeling more joyful, peaceful, calm, and centred. These are great bio-chemical reasons to do it.

The four attitudes focus on four key emotions: appreciation, gratitude, love, and compassion, with the techniques taking you through specific mantras. It's an experiential process that is guided and requires feedback and careful attention to your individual questions and experience. This allows individuals to embody how the attitudes can operate for them, with on-the-spot, personal feedback along the way.

The four attitudes themselves are universal. When building a great leadership practice that people can adopt, that starts to build this sense of safety and community, it all begins with appreciation, the first attitude of the Engagement Wheel.

Create a daily 'four attitudes' practice for yourself. Use your journal or your planning diary to trigger the focus.

- Appreciation: What do I appreciate about myself? My colleagues? My team? My organisation?

- Gratitude: What can I thank myself for? My colleagues? My team? My organisation?

- Love: What do I love about myself? My colleagues? My team? My organisation?

- Compassion: How can I help myself today? My colleagues?

Create and implement a daily 'four attitudes' practice with your team during your daily Touchpoint meeting.

- **Theme word rotation:** You can focus on one attitude per day and get each person to share something from that attitude, in any of the areas (self, colleague, team, or organisation).

- **Out of the hat:** Have one 'hat' (a bowl will do just fine) with each attitude written on a piece of paper. Have a second bowl with each focus area (self, colleague, team, organisation) written on a piece of paper. Each person selects an attitude and a focus and then shares.

- **Love bombs:** Put all the team members' names in a separate hat and choose one. Pick an attitude out of the hat. Now each person shares their love bomb for that that person. For example, you may have chosen 'gratitude' and 'Fred'. Each team member then shares what they are grateful for when it comes to Fred, or something they want to thank him for. Fred gets to receive and say 'thank you' at the end.

D. Common ground

Get to know your people, as people

When we know more about each other, we have less assumptions to push against. We don't need to be best friends with the people we work with. We don't need to hang out with them, or even share the same interests. Yet when we know more about each other as people, we can reach common ground more quickly, keep defensive weapons at bay, and speak directly with respect.

These are some of the topics you can explore with your team, as the occasional way to finish a daily or weekly Touchpoint:

Share with each other:

· Do you have or have you had any pets? What are their names?

· Do you play or follow any sports, teams, or athletes? Which is your favourite or least favourite sport?

· What hobbies do you have?

· Which cities have you visited? Favourite? Least favourite?

· What was your favourite and least favourite subject at school?

· What is your country of origin or number of heritages or languages in the family tree?

· What is your favourite holiday destination?

· What kind of movie do you like? Do you have a favourite actor?

· Do you like reading books? If so, what is your favourite genre or author?

If you want to explore this genre of sharing, you can also try the App *36 Questions*[38]. It's designed to build intimacy and trust between people.

After an unusual and shared experience, simply being together can be very powerful for your team.

---

38   A.D. Adams, *36 Questions V1.0.1*, [mobile application software], retrieved from https://play.google.com

Showcase
Tales of an old sea dog

When working with one organisation in the seafood industry at a yearly Touchpoint, I witnessed the group spontaneously telling their life stories over dinner.

Jeff had worked at the organisation for 30 years. He'd seen many iterations of the problems they were discussing and had a sense that everything comes along in cycles. He said as much, repeatedly. Jeff tended to keep his head down and keep quiet, and wait for the new changes to cycle back to the old ones again.

He had been reluctant to attend the retreat for those reasons. With gentle encouragement from his manager, he agreed to attend. It was against his nature and inclination. To his credit, he showed up, paid attention, and participated. While the issues discussed by the team were still difficult, the overwhelming sense of commitment and focus was there. The Team Compass helped them to have common ground of core beliefs.

At dinner, a lot of the more difficult issues had been tabled. The stories began, with the CEO going first. He shared some of his more difficult roles in the industry. He also told of his joy in becoming a grandfather and how much he adores his wife of 40 years. Others followed suit, revealing different adventures prior to their current workplace.

Then it was Jeff's turn. He'd started in the industry as a scientist. He talked extensively about his love of the ocean, the miracle of sea life, and the unbounded nature of that environment and the depths of the seas as yet unexplored.

I watched the others as they listened spellbound to Jeff's tale. The delight in his subject matter brightened his often impassive face, and his passion reeled them in. We saw at last the man behind the professional veneer. One of his colleagues said later, "Now I know why Jeff is so stubborn about some issues. It's not that he dislikes change, it's that he knows what some change can mean to the future of the sea and its creatures. And he sees it as his life's mission to protect that which can never be replaced if we get it wrong."

Jeff went from being perceived as a stick-in-the-mud old-timer to the individual who embodied the north point on the Team Compass – what they valued most, the sea.

Implement

How well do you know your people? Do you know what is important to them? What lights them up? What they care about? How well do your people know you? Are you accessible? Do you share your trials and triumphs...or do you over-share?

1. Compile a list of 'get to know you' topics with your team. Use the ones included here, or the ones shared in 36 Questions.

2. At one of your daily or weekly Touchpoints, pull one of the questions from the hat and share.

3. In your one-to-one engagements, check in with people and find out how they are doing, as people.

Part 3

Talk

Four leadership conversations for growth

The biggest stumbling block to success as a leader and as a team is the ability to have leadership conversations. Being able to raise issues, give feedback, explore ideas, challenge authority, and have constructive disagreements is vital to a healthy and forward-moving team. The leader's role is to create the environment where people feel safe to have these conversations.

Connection really is currency in leadership. The capacity to engage and discuss is what unleashes ideas, it's what builds relationships and trust, and it's what creates reputations. If we can't connect, we can't influence. And if we can't influence, we can't lead. Leadership conversations must be mastered to ensure connection – to engage head, heart, hands, and soul.

There are four types of leadership conversations. These are:

· **Performance Conversations**, which are about delivery. They are about getting the job done well. When it comes to work, this is about our *hands*.

· **Engagement Conversations**, which are about relationships. It's about how we interact and relate as people. These kinds of conversations are all about the *heart*.

· **Challenge Conversations**, which are about beliefs. In these conversations we go deep into who we are, what we believe, and whether that aligns with what is being expressed in the organisation. These kinds of conversations are about the *soul*.

· **Collaboration Conversations**, which are about ideas. This is the realm typically associated with leadership: vision, direction, innovation. These kinds of conversations are very much about the *head*, and then flow into engaging heart, soul, and hands.

———◆———

Performance Conversations: Hands

As leaders, our main role is to ensure that we and our team get the tools of the job and produce the work that we are meant to, to a quality that meets or exceeds expectations. Sometimes things don't go as planned, and folks don't deliver on what is expected. We need to know how to course correct with people, as well as keep them on track when things are going well.

The language of feedback

The ability to provide genuine and constructive feedback is critical for any team to progress towards a more robust culture. So many of us struggle with this skill! We often experience constructive feedback as a survival threat. It goes to that basic fear of feeling rejected or unworthy, and disappointing others. We can feel ashamed and embarrassed as a result. Delivering that feedback can be just as traumatising. To be the harbinger of bad news is an unpleasant task. What we need is to transform is our *relationship* with feedback. Feedback helps us grow and expand our perspective. It is a true gift to be savoured.

Yet we often shirk feedback. Sometimes this is because of the way it is delivered. If the other person is weird about giving it, it makes us feel weird too. They waffle around the issue and then finally blurt it out. It's not so much what they said as how long they've been sitting on it. They worry about it, mull it over, and it fills their mind and soul with judgments and frustrations.

Why do we do keep quiet when something needs to be said? Is it because we don't want to make someone else suffer, or it could be that when someone does something that irritates us, it launches an internal dialogue of judgment that wells up from our inner being like molten effluent. These judgments come from a huge reservoir of life experiences that helps filter new experiences for threat or safety. It's our shortcut thinking that helps us make decisions quickly about situations and relationships, assessing them for threat or safety in a blink of an eye.[39]

---

39   Daniel Kahneman wrote brilliantly about this in *Thinking, Fast and Slow*, London,

It does, however, get us into trouble when our perception differs from that of others. This is why cross-cultural training is so important: it allows us to learn about social norms that we have no reference or context for. If there is an inadvertent trespass, we don't know about it until someone has the courtesy to tell us. All feedback ought to be done this way: as a courtesy to let someone else know their action is being received in a negative context.

Showcase
Limit your footprint

We were visiting friends for a week. Wary of overstepping the limits of hospitality, I asked my friend on the first day about house rules and if there was anything we should avoid doing to not upset home harmony. She said, "As long as you don't play loud music at 4am, we're all good." She had a beautiful spacious house and made us feel right at home.

That was until the night before we were leaving, when it all came out. It turns out she was only just tolerating our presence. I was horrified! I asked what we could to make things easier on her, and she said, "Reduce your footprint. Don't spread out so much." I sat in stunned silence. It never occurred to me that we were spreading out or taking over the space. We had shoes at the door, towels on the line, food in the kitchen, and a suitcase in the study because it did not fit in the spare room. It wasn't that much. But there were little bits of our stuff in their space.

Having lived communally in several different organisations, at summer camp and at Outward Bound, I'd developed a more tolerant threshold for shared space, and had no idea that these things would irk someone else. The worst part about it was that I had asked at the beginning if there was anything to do or not to do. I had invited feedback!

And that's the thing. Many of us would rather whinge privately than address the uncomfortable aspect of a difficult conversation. Meanwhile I would much rather have known at the beginning of our visit that our behaviour was causing irritation. I had no idea, and therefore no ability to redress or stop the irritation.

Penguin, 2011. Malcolm Gladwell's book *Blink – The Power of Thinking Without Thinking*, London, Penguin, 2005, is also excellent.

My colleague and I have an agreement. If either of us does something that treads on the other's toes, then we are to speak up about it immediately. For us, it is far worse for the other person to grind an axe behind our back and not give us the opportunity to make things better. That way we know our relationship is always genuine. We raise issues and deal with them. This is because we respect each other enough to get over the discomfort of sharing something that bothers us.

We use the following rules:

- Assume no ill intention
- We would rather know than not
- Feedback is an opportunity to expand perspective
- Feedback is a courtesy, not a chastisement.

What to keep in mind when giving feedback

There is a science and an art to giving feedback. Here are some things to consider:

Timing: Be mindful of what else is going on for you and for the other person. You don't want to add tension to a person before they are about to deliver an important speech for example, or about to go in to meet their manager for a promotion. Nor do you want to leave it too long, lest it become a festering boil that explodes at an even less opportune moment.

Environment: Be mindful of privacy. Also be mindful of power plays; you want to be on neutral territory, if possible.

Preparation: Consider your **real** intention for giving the message. Write out any judgments that sit with the feedback that are making it challenging for you to share.

Language: Wherever possible, use 'I' language. Phrase the observations from your perspective instead of loading defensiveness in to a series of 'you did this/you said that' messages.

Balance positive and negative: What happens when every time you see a dog you give it a kick? Pretty soon the dog learns to shy away from you and hide. People can be like that too. We experience constructive feedback as a little bit of pain, even if it is in our own best interest. If all we ever get from a manager are little corrections, then we start to flinch every time that manager approaches us. So as leaders, we need to think about a 3:1 ratio of positive to negative. We want to reinforce what is going well and right so that our team members seek to repeat that behaviour. This is a positive reinforcement loop. Then where there is corrective feedback to be given, it does not feel so damaging, as we have plenty of other evidence about what we are doing well. One piece of criticism does not bring down the confidence we have if the majority of our work is going well.

Dialogues

The feedback formula for correcting behaviour

Feedback needs to be a conversation. It is not uni-directional. Uni-directional feedback is a directive, or a request to honour boundaries. We will talk about boundaries in just a moment. Meanwhile, feedback is an exploration of perspective with the objective of building a shared understanding of the best way forward on an issue. This issue is usually around behaviour and how it is interpreted by others.

1. Check your intentions first

To deliver feedback, first get very clear on your intentions. Get real with yourself about what you are actually trying to achieve. Are you pissed off because someone upset you and you want to have a little dig at them? Are you lashing out in anger, frustration or pain of some sort? If so, then stop! These are not good intentions. The only worthy intention in delivering feedback is the one where you want to preserve or improve a performance and/or relationship. With this higher intention in mind, you will be less emotionally volatile and better able to stay away from aggressive or passive-aggressive behaviour.

2. Situation

Start with a statement of fact. This is something that happened that you both know has happened.

In this example, the business owner of a retail shop has found a staff member reading behind the counter, yet again. The business owner has already asked the staff member not to do this and explained the two main reasons: it gives the impression of idleness to customers if they come in, and there is always something to do in the shop. The staff member acknowledged the feedback at the time. Since then the business owner has caught the staff member reading a book yet again. This is the third such occasion.

Example: "Susan, when I came in to the shop today I saw that you were reading your book again behind the service counter."

They both know this to be true because on the two previous occasions the business owner had raised the issue with the staff member.

3. Impact

Explain the impact, according to your observations, thoughts, and feelings.

Example: "I felt frustrated by this as it is the third time I have found you reading since I first asked you not to a few months ago. I still think it gives a bad impression to customers. I also know there is a lot to do in the store. When I see you reading I feel disappointed because I have asked you not do it previously, explained the reasons why, and the work in the shop is not getting done."

4. Invite

This is the interaction part. You invite their perspective.

Example: "We may have a difference of perspective here and I may be missing something. Can you tell me what is going on for you in the shop? What are your expectations when it is quiet?"

If, like me, you just want to shout at Susan and ask, 'Why do you continue to defy me?', then know that this will only result in defensiveness. There is still an opportunity to turn this around, or at least to get insight in to the blocks to performance behaviour. It could be that Susan does not know what tasks need to be done and does not have the same initiative and task-seeking eye as a business owner. These things often need to be taught. It could be that Susan does not know how to do some tasks, even though she knows they need to be done. So the problem might be in training, or in not creating an environment where staff feel safe to ask for help.

Or maybe Susan is a defiant slacker.

Only go to the very last conclusion after you have exhausted and explored all other avenues of what it is you are doing, or not doing, that is creating poor performance. Often the fault in performance is in the systems or in the manager for not explaining things correctly. Assume that someone's poor performance may stem from something you have or haven't done as their manager. This keeps you from jumping at them in frustration and invites them to a collaborative conversation.

5. Suggest

The 'invite' step is the meat of the conversation. The two of you explore perspectives, possible lacks in performance, and figure out what could be done to improve the situation. The 'suggest' part of the formula is where you put forward your specific suggestions on what you would like to see improved. So if the collaborative conversation fails to deliver ideas from the other person, you've got some suggestions ready to go. Always agree to check back in within an appropriate time frame, depending on circumstance. The sooner the better, to reinforce what is going well.

The feedback formula for positive reinforcement

This works just the same way. In this scenario, Rob has cooked an extraordinary dinner. Zoë wants to reinforce this behaviour in the hope of many more fine meals being cooked for her by her loving husband.

1. Intention

I genuinely wanted to show appreciation and reinforce a job well done.

2. Situation

"Rob, you outdid yourself tonight! The salmon is perfectly cooked, the veggies are crisp and delicious, and the little chocolate mousse you whipped up is amazing."

3. Impact

"I feel completely spoiled! I am a happy wife!"

4. Invite

"What inspired you to go the extra mile tonight? Were you following a recipe or making it up?"

5. Suggest

"I think it would be a great idea for you to cook every night so you can develop your culinary skills even further."

Rob may see through my attempt to get out of cooking duty in this last suggestion. However, by giving genuine feedback in this way we get to explore the recipe for success and highlight the positive impact of good behaviour – with much benefit to me!

The feedback formula to establish good boundaries

These are one-way directives explaining how you wish to be treated, and why. It has elements of feedback in it as we share how certain behaviours make us feel. This is a useful framework when there seems to be an imbalance of power between the person putting a boundary in place, and the other person. Boundaries are good when we feel less powerful than the person we are talking to.

In contrast, the feedback formula works well from a position of power to someone in a less powerful position.

What to say in expressing a boundary that you want to be honoured by someone in a more powerful position:

When you...

I feel...

Instead, please…

Example: A CEO has been on the receiving end of a lot of criticism. It seems all the conversations with the Chair of the Board are unconstructive and harsh. The CEO decides that there is a need for a more balanced approach:

"George, whenever we meet you start the conversation with a criticism. I feel the negativity continues throughout the conversation and I feel a little attacked. I feel the conversation is a little unbalanced. Instead, I'd appreciate if we could include focus on what is going well, not just what is going wrong. Is that ok with you?"

What the CEO does well is to highlight the impact, 'feeling attacked'. He softens the feedback with 'a little', to keep the Chair from becoming defensive, and to manage his own emotional responses. The CEO does not make the other person wrong, and does not ask George to drop the criticism, only to include positive focus as well to balance it out.

Implement

So let's do a little self-reflection.

On a scale of 1-5, what is your confidence level or competence level with:

- Giving constructive feedback?
- Giving positive feedback?
- Resolving relationship issues?

Feedback reflection:

- What is the best feedback you have ever received?
- What made it good?
- What is the worst feedback you have ever received?
- What made it bad?
- What are your fears about feedback?

- What feedback do you need to give that you are currently avoiding? Why?
- Who can you approach to give you honest and caring feedback about your performance in the workplace?

Performance conversations are often about the past and what's happened. It would be far more beneficial to focus on the future instead. Here's the coaching questions you can use to frame the whole experience of your performance conversations.

Reflection – learning from the past

- What did you learn?
- What did you achieve?
- What did you fail at?
- Who did you help?
- Who did you ask for help?
- What values did you embrace?
- What behaviours did you demonstrate to support the Team Compass?
- What are you proud of?
- What do you regret?
- What's next?

Projection – framing the future

- It's three months from now. What do you expect to be doing/seeing/saying/hearing/feeling?
- What do we need to do/learn to experience that?

Engagement Conversations: Heart

The language of relationships

To be able to apologise when things go wrong, or when we make a mistake that affects others negatively, is hard work. These are the difficult skills of interpersonal engagement. How we nurture and manage our relationships is one of the secrets to successful long-term leadership.

We're going to take a deep dive on the art of apologising. If anything gets in the way of healthy work relationships, it's when an apology is due but is withheld. As leaders, we need to be able to express remorse and regret, and to make amends. It signals humility and compassion, and not being exempt from common decency. Done right, an apology repairs and builds relationships.

Showcase: Apology to the Stolen Generations

Steve is a young man I mentored for a while. He discovered late in his teens that he is of Aboriginal heritage. His mother and father had kept the family background a secret, which was a hangover from the Stolen Generations of the early-1900s through to the 1970s. Being Aboriginal meant you were at risk of being taken from your family, and at the time there was shame and fear attached to Aboriginal identity.

Steve was amazed and delighted to discover this part of himself, then deeply sad at the irreparable loss of language and culture that had fallen through the cracks. Thousands of years of heritage and lore about the land, about relationships and ancestry, has disappeared without the continuous cultural education program Aboriginal people had conducted over some 60,000 years. All gone in a few decades.

In 2008, then Prime Minister Kevin Rudd read an official apology to the Aboriginal families[40] affected by the forcible removal of children from Aboriginal homes under the Commonwealth, state and territory Aboriginal protection and welfare laws and policies. These removals

---

40   Read more about the Apology to Australia's Indigenous peoples at The Australian Institute of Aboriginal and Torres Strait Islander Studies.

are known as the Stolen Generations. It was an acknowledgement of suffering and an intention to make amends.

Forcible removable of children from their families into state or religious care affected Aboriginal communities around Australia. The policy was to socialise and integrate them completely into mainstream Australian culture. They were often forbidden to speak their native language. This is how much of the erosion of culture and community was accelerated. Many Aboriginal people have never found their birth families.

The Apology was an incredibly moving experience to witness. The palpable sense of loss and grief was a wound etched into the country's soul. And now with an official apology, that grievous wound could see daylight and be given a chance to breathe and heal. The gaping sense of loss stretched like a dark chasm all around us. Acknowledgment of this irreversible devastation allowed us to pause and consider, "What now, given all that pain? How can we help our brothers and sisters make a new life through this?"

It won't bring back lost family connections or the years that were taken from parents and children. It won't bring back the lost languages, the lost traditions, or the ceremonial rituals that died out with the last of the elders before they were able to initiate their kin properly. While an apology cannot undo what was done, it can nurture the seeds of healing. Acknowledging pain and suffering is a message of respect and compassion. It says, "I acknowledge that harm was done to you and for that I feel sorrow. And I want to help make it better if I can."

How to apologise

The best way to apologise is to realise first that there is something to apologise for. That's half the battle. Sometimes we can get really caught up in our own inner dialogue and justification for our actions.

But our sense of guilt is a dead giveaway. When we come face-to-face with our own complicity in someone else's pain, it can mean a strong sense of shame for us. Shame is one of the most powerful negative emotions we can experience. We will do a lot to protect ourselves from shame, and may end up lying or blaming others, justifying our actions or making excuses.

Timing

It takes real courage to front up and acknowledge that we have done the wrong thing. When we really don't want to apologise and we're hiding out, then this is the best moment to say sorry. As soon as we realise that we need to apologise, that's the time to apologise.

Take ownership

The first step in an apology is to acknowledge that we've done something wrong. Describe exactly what we did and get the facts on the table. This is a great starting point. We need to acknowledge why this particular behaviour was wrong and that it violated a moral imperative. The second step is an explanation. This is not making excuses. It is simply revealing the context of our behaviour and decision-making at the time. The next part of the explanation is to acknowledge where the logic and behaviour was flawed. And what we have learned from it as a result.

Be sorry

Another key aspect of an apology is to express real remorse. To actually feel regret that we caused harm. We can't fake this. We have to embody it. And we need to share that deep pain with the other person.

Reparations

The last part of an apology is about making amends. It's not good enough just to end with "I'm really sorry" and to cry a little. The next part is asking, "How do I make this right and help make it better?" It is a way of inviting collaboration and repairing the relationship. It gives us an opportunity to demonstrate good faith and our intention to change our behaviour.

What to expect after you apologise

The short answer to that is: nothing. Saying sorry with an expectation of forgiveness in return is without sincerity. An apology given with respect is enough of an act itself. We have no control over whether or not somebody accepts our apology. So for peace of mind, know that we have done our best to repair the damage that was done.

In return, forgiving a person is something that we can take ownership of. Holding onto a grievance is like holding onto a burning ember with a clenched fist. And forgiveness is not condoning any action by others. It's deciding to let go of the past as a way of defining the present. It's accepting what happened and choosing to create something new with our life.

Implement

The quality of our relationships determines professional success. Saying sorry is definitely challenging. Let's do some personal reflection.

- Remember a time when you apologised to someone. How did it feel beforehand? During? Afterwards?

- What did you do well?

- What could have been done better?

- What was your intention in apologising?

- Did you feel like you made amends?

Challenge Conversations: Soul

The language of beliefs

One of the most difficult situations we can find ourselves in is when we fundamentally disagree with decisions or behaviours that are happening in the workplace.

These are not so much about a difference of opinion on where the office party should be held, but on more substantive, values-based issues. They are tough, because they cause us to explore the core of who we are, what we stand for, and what we are prepared to risk to challenge the status quo and rock the boat.

When we stand up for our beliefs, we stand out. There is a lot at stake when we challenge: reputation, relationships, belonging, alliances, security. Thank goodness it's not often that we come up against a soul-testing issue! I wrote extensively about these situations, these 'rock and a hard place' experiences, in my second book *Moments*[41]. In facing these difficult moments, we need to consider the action or lack of it against our own personal values, the impact it had on others, and what would happen if indeed everyone did what we did (or did not do). More familiar challenges are when we need to challenge the status quo and consider slaying some sacred cows.

How to challenge the status quo

Status quo is the existing state of affairs. As a species, we can get accustomed to many things. The uncomfortable familiar is more comfortable than the unfamiliar. In other words, we get used to what we know. We put up with faulty systems, archaic processes, or cumbersome rituals because 'that's the way it's done around here'. This is incredibly infuriating for new people who haven't yet adjusted to the awkwardness of the default, and may in fact have experience doing things differently in a better, faster, more efficient and effective way. Remember that new staff are a huge opportunity for a business.

---

41   Z. Routh, *Moments – Leadership when it matters most*, Canberra, Inner Compass Australia Pty Ltd, 2016.

The first 100 days

For a new staff member, the first 100 days are a golden opportunity to use their fresh eyes on the status quo. Unlike the US presidency, where the expectation is that the first 100 days will set the tone for the remainder of the term, the first 100 days for new staff should be a time for observing, asking questions, and finding out why things happen the way they do and what the legacy is behind them. Task new staff with collecting their observations, questions, and suggestions in that time frame. Their insight is enlightening and could lead to breakthrough changes in performance and engagement.

If you do not have any new staff to lean on, plan an exercise with your team. Imagine that you have an alien from outer space visiting your workplace. You need to explain to that alien what you are doing and why you are doing it. It's amazing what emerges when you have to showcase defaults and make sense of them. Some of them do not make sense at all.

How to slay a sacred cow

The expression 'sacred cow' relates to the Hindu belief that cows are sacred animals. Their milk produces nourishment for mothers, babies, and the whole family, so they are seen as a sacred life-giving mother. Cows take priority on Indian roads and in villages. They are not slaughtered or eaten by Hindus, and it is considered very bad luck to hit and kill a cow with your vehicle.

In the workplace, sacred cows are so elevated in the psyche of the organisation that they are beyond criticism. Sometimes these sacred cows are deemed to be venerated unreasonably, and conflict in the workplace can result. Sacred cows can be trivial (such as no-one can use the boss's mug), while others have larger implications (such as the project that will save the day but has not delivered results in years).

Rules, rituals, and attitudes become sacred cows because of the emotional attachment to them. It could be related to reputation, pride, nostalgia, or identity. Killing the sacred cow feels like a huge loss and a threat. Sometimes it's hard to face up to the reality that things are changing, and that we need to adapt.

Showcase
The spaghetti chart

In a workplace years ago, my colleagues felt like they were in a process abyss. They were frustrated at not being able to get things changed, it was unclear to whom to make suggestions, how those suggestions were assessed, and what happened to the decision as a result. It was deflating.

A project officer was tasked with capturing the existing process. The result was a flowchart that looked like mangled spaghetti. It was so ridiculous that we framed it. The organisation had become so risk averse, so bogged down with protocol, that it was virtually paralysed by its processes.

From suggestions for improvements to the lunch menu through to streamlining preparations for client programs, they all went through the spaghetti. By the time the idea had worked its way through the process, if it moved at all, the staff member had either moved on or given up. Basically, nothing changed.

The 'spaghetti chart' inspired a staff meeting where we staged a sacred cow hunting initiative. All staff were invited to share what they felt was getting in the way, slowing us down, and not adding value. Little things and big things went up on that list. Everything from the shoe policy (having to wear closed toe shoes on the property, even on a day off in your own accommodation), to leave approvals, to program and task allocation, to how to get a promotion, to complaining without making suggestions for improvements.

Many of those cows got taken out for slaughter that day. Others took longer to address. Things changed. Things got better, spirits lifted, and productivity soared.

Prepare for resistance

Change can be both disruptive and exciting, depending on perception and what is valued by the people affected. If change is being initiated without any input, then resistance is more likely. Consultation and transparency about the decision-making process help demystify it.

Be lighthearted about change. At Mitel Corp some 20 years ago, their leaders went on a sacred cow hunting expedition, and then made it a new expectation: if you see something that does not add value or slows the team down, get rid of it. Outside the Head of Quality's office was a life-sized wooden cow. They had cow postcards, calendars, and figurines. They made it fun to address the issues.[42]

Implement

Spotting the status quo:

List assumptions that you have about your work, career, boss, and colleagues.

Now reverse them.

Explore the limitations in your thinking:

- I could never....earn/learn
- I would never...
- I can't...
- I won't...
- I should...

What reality are you basing these on? What would happen if you changed all these negatives to positives?

Sacred Cow tipping:

What sacred cows do you have in your workplace?

What would happen if you removed that cow? What are the possible repercussions?

Who supports the sacred cow and why?

Can the sacred cow sentiment be preserved in some other way?

What is the sacred cow costing you?

---

42   See D. Beardlsey, 'This Company Doesn't Brake for (Sacred) Cows', Fast Company, 31 July, 1998.

Collaboration Conversations: Head

The language of ideas

This is where leadership skills come into their own. Most leaders I first work with have never been taught how to do 'big picture' leadership thinking. Initially they leave a lot to gut instinct, logic, and their experience. Mostly this serves them well, until they grow stagnant and ideas feel stale.

There are critical skills to master for collaboration conversations. First you need the basics of managing meetings to develop and assess ideas. These are the fundamentals of good facilitation, and include an agenda with the outcomes and process identified. You need to make sure you focus on one type of a meeting at a time.

There are three types of collaborative meeting:

1. Information sharing
2. Decision-making
3. Idea generating

Information sharing meetings need to be killed off. This is a common sacred cow in business practices that does not add value and wastes time. With technology there are far better ways to inform people about progress on projects, give important updates, and so on.

Decision-making and idea generating meetings can be incorporated into one of your Touchpoint meetings, depending on the scope and scale of what needs to be addressed. Decision-making meetings need to have clear parameters and sufficient information for all parties to make a meaningful contribution. There are many different ways to assess the choices in decision-making. I recommend *The Decision Book – 50 models for strategic thinking*[43]. It covers everything from how to understand yourself and others better, to how to identify the next big thing, and how to identify a gap in the market.

---

43   M. Krogerus and R. Tschäppeler, *The Decision Book – 50 models for strategic thinking*, London, Profile Books, 2011. Your shortcut to looking brilliant. Go nuts.

Idea generating benefits

When you facilitate idea-generating conversations you can:

- Apply creative thinking techniques to wicked problems and pervasive business challenges
- Collaborate and innovate together
- Inspire others
- Guide and coach colleagues, rather than command or control
- Communicate with persuasion to motivate and convince others
- Advocate for your own and others' ideas.

A team that generates ideas together bonds together. The key premise that underpins successful collaborative conversations and the language of ideas is this concept:

New thoughts don't pop out of nowhere; they are generated by applying filters to our thinking.

Strategic thinking is largely done ad hoc, even when a team commits an entire weekend to the activity. What usually happens is that people jostle for their favourite project aligned against the key goals. The loudest often succeeds, while many ideas fade quietly away.

Effective collaborative conversations that generate new, powerful strategy apply filters and lenses to their thinking. It is the structure and restriction of filters that paradoxically allow for the flow of new ideas. Think of how a river increases in force when it is dammed and then released: the potential force of that water is funnelled powerfully for others' use. Thinking with filters allow us to do that. The filters clean up our thinking and funnel it towards a powerful focus.

There are many different types of filters to apply to your collaborative conversations. These include:

- Ecosystems
- Scenarios
- Mapping
- Creative

Think in ecosystems

One of the hallmarks of effective strategy is its consideration of complexity. Organisations today are awash in many different pressures and systems. Leaders who can map ecosystems and bring to the surface the challenges and opportunities of even the most dense and multifaceted situations.

Ecosystems don't exist only in the natural world. They exist in social, technological, economic, political, and organisational contexts. Each of these ecosystems interacts with others to form an overarching context for the leader, their team, and organisation. Mapping the dynamics of these ecosystems makes visible the forces at play that may help or hinder the team and organisational goals.

How to map ecosystems:

- First, take a large piece of paper or draw on a whiteboard.

- Start with the organisation at the centre of the map, represented as a circle or another shape.

- Ask: What are the key organisational factors that are shaping the organisation from within? This is thinking about the organisation as an ecosystem in itself. Some examples include: Board and CEO relationship, executive team dynamics, operations and marketing relationship, point-of-sale systems, new products being implemented. Draw each factor as a bubble attached to the main organisational bubble.

- Next, move on to the other relevant ecosystems (social, technological, economic, environmental, political) that are affecting the organisation and its progress.

- Draw lines to either the organisational bubble or to its sub-bubbles. Draw the connections as influencing forces, with directional or multidirectional arrows. You now have the rudimentary beginnings of a systems map. [44]

---

44 This is an advanced leadership thinking skill. I recommend Peter Senge et al., *The Fifth Discipline Fieldbook – Strategies and Tools for Building a Learning Organization*, New York, Doubleday, 1994.

- From here you will be able to consider where the hotspots of activity are. These are the spots that have a lot of inbound arrows and pressures, and the bubbles that have a lot of outbound influence. The former are a point of effect and possible weakness. The latter, the ones with outbound arrows, are points of influence and potential areas for intervention. In looking at these, consider, "Do we have influence here? Could we get influence here? What can we do to manage these points of influence if not?".

Plan in scenarios

A shorthand for this style of thinking filter is the 'best-case and worst-case scenario' concept. We think, "What happens if it all goes perfectly?" and then, "What if it all goes completely wrong?". This allows us to prepare for both situations and feel less anxious as a result. Advanced scenario planning takes a different tack. It's about creating four possible futures for the team and organisation, and making plans based on those four possible worlds.

It starts with identifying the most major volatile trends affecting the organisation (as above, these might be social, technological, environmental, economic, political, or organisational). The key is to focus next on the trends that could go either way, not ones that we know are already heading in one particular direction. For example, in the university sector, one of their key most volatile trends is public funding. The government of the day can change its approach to public tertiary education funding within an election cycle of three years, and funding could increase or decrease depending on the priorities of the current government. This makes long-term planning extremely difficult for institutions committed to four-year degrees. University leaders would be wise to include funding as one of their significant trends to consider.

Once you have a handful of trends identified, choose the two most volatile and relevant ones. Now you get to draw a quadrant, with one trend taking the horizontal axis and the other the vertical one. You now have the beginnings of four possible worlds. Look at the intersection of each corner and talk through the possible outcomes in that world if those trends played out. For example, in the university sector you might have decreased public funding and a decline in demand for key programs due to industry disruption. In this possible world, the university might be facing significant decrease in revenue and demand. The team might choose to label this scenario 'Doomsday' or something similar. Continue with each of the quadrants until you have all of the worlds labelled, with some dot points about what that world might look like.

Now you can start making plans. Focus on what you can do to bring to light your favourite possible world, and what you can do to avoid the others, or at least prepare for such an eventuality.

Map energy

A great way to assess the engagement energy that you have in a team or organisation is to draw a heat map, or social diagram. In this process, you create a mind map or connecting bubbles as you did previously with the ecosystems, except this time you focus on individuals and map out their connections. Who is each person close to? Who are the influencers? Who is on the outside? This way you can start to see the unofficial interactions and how messages and ideas can be floated or seeded throughout an organisation.

The energy map also allows you to see where problems may arise. These might be cliques or loners that need to be brought into the fold, or at the very least need a conversation to find out how they're feeling and thinking. The conversations so far have been diagnostic: getting to an understanding of the forces at play in your given context. The next set of collaborative conversations are about generating new ideas around these complex situations.

Key principles for collaboration and creative thinking conversations

Divergent thinking is creating and discovering new ideas and connections.

Convergent thinking is deciding which idea is the best.

Most leaders do a lot of convergent thinking without doing any divergent thinking first. They recycle old ideas and are blind to biases and habits.

When to use creative thinking skills for collaborative conversations

When you're stuck: This could be a persistent problem – a large-scale intractable challenge. Or maybe a circular problem, where you keep seeing this problem come up again and again, cyclically or seasonally.

When you want to launch something new: This could be a new product, service, program, or even career.

When you want to improve performance: This could be team performance or to meet a bold new target, sales performance, or leadership performance.

Implement

Draw a rudimentary ecosystem map of the forces at play in your world

This will reveal the complexity and opportunities that exist in your current context.

Create a scenario plan

Identify two major trends, with unknown outcomes that could go either way (increase or decrease, improve or worsen). Name the quadrants and identify some possible features of that world. Identify three actions that you can take to best respond and plan for each of the worlds.

Map the energy in the team and organisation

Draw a mind map of the relationships you observe in your team and the organisation. Ask, 'Where is the most influence? What are the groups that hold power? How are the relationships between other individuals and groups?'

Choose a challenge and apply one of the following techniques to start generating new ideas.

1. Think in threes

Two ideas create binaries. Three ideas force new connections.

2. Problem Tree

Start with your central problem at the top of the page. Then draw two branches down from it, each with a contributing problem. Draw two more branches down from each of the second layer for problems that contributed to each of those. You can go for a third layer. Now review each branch and look for where you can intervene to solve aspects of the challenge. Sometimes it helps to start with smaller down-the-tree problems, and these can lead to solving the problems further up the tree.

3. Use a different lens

Pick a letter out of the alphabet. List three professions or roles that start with that letter (for example the letter 'B' might have 'Baker', 'Banker', and 'Brother'). Now make a list of suggestions about your challenge, based on the perspective of these different roles.

4. Consult your imaginary Board of Directors

Pick five people, living or dead, whom you admire greatly in any field (think business, family, religious, spiritual, scientific, or political). Imagine them at a Board meeting with you. One-by-one, imagine asking their opinion on how you should tackle this particular problem.

Conclusion

Leadership is an honour and a privilege. To be a steward of people and a cause, and create results for the people we serve, is a responsibility not to be taken lightly. It requires persistence. It demands self-examination. It can cause the greatest pain as well as the greatest joy.

In all of our best efforts to create a workplace worth belonging to, to be a leader worth following, we may yet be faced with that moment when a good and trusted staff member says, "I'm going".

The way we make that moment better is through knowing in our heart of hearts that we did our best. We created a safe place to work. We fostered robust team spirit. We followed our Team Compass and honoured our values. We built a cadence of interactions with our own unique rituals, with highs and lows and peak moments to be savoured as precious memories. We had the hard conversations. We went head-to-head with our beliefs and assumptions. We dug into new ideas and made new things come to life.

Loyalty begins with us, the leaders. How we show up and how we shape the work and our relationships determines the outcome. Loyalty is ultimately the bond that exists between people, purpose, and place. We have a calling and an opportunity to make that bond a rich and wonderful experience, long after people have left the organisation.

In Buddhist practice, nothing lasts forever, and attachment is the path to suffering. And yet what endures for leaders is striving to create the environment and experiences that foster growth and commitment. Hold on tightly with an open palm.

When that team member hands in their notice, you can look them in the eye and know that you did your best for them. And you'll know too that they did their best for you, and for the team. It's a farewell, not a goodbye, for in what you co-created with your team, you know that you shared amazing experiences and that the loyalty you shared lives on as advocacy.

I wish you well in your leadership journey as you sail ever onwards on your adventures, boundless, in good company.

About the author

Zoë Routh is a leadership mentor and speaker. English born, Canadian raised, Australian adopted, Outdoor Adventurist and Experiential Educator, Truth Teller, Learner, Cancer Dancer, One-Time Belly Dancer, Aspiring Telemark Skiier, Slayer of Dragons, Mother of Chickens.

From the wild rivers of northern Ontario to the remote regions of Australia, Zoë has spent the last 30 years showing people how to work together better.

She began her career leading canoe trips through the rugged Canadian wilderness. In 1996 she moved to Australia to work with Outward Bound, where she developed nationally recognised outdoor leadership training programs. Furthering her passion for people and learning, she developed leadership programs for rural sector industries such as wine, rice, and mining for the Australian Rural Leadership Foundation.

She is obsessed with showing big thinkers with big hearts how to make a big difference. Zoë works closely with senior leaders in higher education, the private sector, rural industry groups, and the public service. Her high-impact leadership learning programs take place indoors and outdoors in spectacular settings.

As a high-energy and engaging speaker, she presents frequently to industry groups and organisations about loyalty and leadership.

Zoë is the author of *Composure – How centred leaders make the biggest impact*, and *Moments – Leadership when it matters most*.

Read more about Zoë's work at www.zoerouth.com

Bonus material

Companion downloads

See www.zoerouth.com/loyalty-bonus to download and listen to your bonus *Loyalty* material.

Podcast interviews:

Sarah Riegelhuth, finance expert, entrepreneur, and author of *Get Rich Slow*

Craig Cherry, customer service expert and Director of The Loyalty Zone

Megan Bromley, former Head of Employee Experience at RedBalloon

How to stop turnover in small to medium enterprises

Downloads include:

Team Compass template

Boundless Teams checklist

Touchpoint Cadence planner and agendas

Next steps

Staying inspired and focused is a discipline. It's easier when you have company! Here are some inspirational and practical ways to build your boundless leadership capacities with Zoë Routh.

www.zoerouth.com

The Blog: Inspiring articles to share and encourage leaders to be their best in the moments that matter.

The Podcast: The Zoë Routh Leadership Podcast keeps you evolving while you drive or slog it out on the treadmill.

The Tube: The Zoë Routh Leadership Moments YouTube channel to nudge your leadership evolution.

Connect:

www.facebook.com/zoe.routh

www.linkedin.com/in/zoerouth

@zoerouth

@zoerouth

Executive Coaching – Boundless Leadership

Zoë shows leaders how to lead with grace. Together, you focus on depth of thinking, effectiveness of action, and quality of presence. Various programs are tailored to you, depending on your stage of leadership development and sphere of influence.

Leader's Edge Mastermind

Zoë's Mastermind training with executive coaching and quarterly training intensives starts with a four-day expedition in a beautiful location such as the Larapinta Trail near Alice Springs, Australia, or the Freycinet Peninsula, Tasmania. Senior leaders come together in inspiring locations to create the time and space for quality reflection and planning for business and self-development. Under the stars and sun, the Leader's Edge Mastermind is about connection, reflection, and traction.

Boundless Teams

Workshops and development programs for new teams, re-formed teams, or ambitious powerhouse teams. Zoë combines the wisdom of the wilderness with the cauldron of the classroom to help teams get real with each other. Leaders will experience collaborative conversations and relationships to advance the work that inspires you. This is how we can put the principles of *Loyalty* into practice!

Acknowledgments

I am deeply grateful for the support I have in my world. This includes my mentors through Thought Leaders Business School. In particular Craig Cherry, Peter Cook, and Matt Church have been instrumental in sharpening my thinking and awakening a courageous heart.

Rachel Bourke and Colin Eggins: thanks so much for stretching my thinking and helping me to play a bigger game in service to leaders worldwide.

My team, Bianca Jurd and Krystal Rochford, for egging me on as much as keeping the ship floating with your attention to client support. Without you, none of our projects and ideas would have gotten off the ground.

A big thank you to Steve, Bron, and Max for hosting me in their awesome home while I wrote a big chunk of this book.

To my amazing clients, the work you do and the courage you show for daring to lead and learn, this is what inspires me and helps me to venture beyond the horizon as well. You are making a profound difference in the world.

To my husband Rob, who keeps me humble and grounded. I look forward to you reminding me of the messages in this book, like you have with *Composure* and *Moments*. You keep me honest and laughing! Life is one grand adventure with you!

To you the reader, for persisting to the end, and for letting these ideas find a home. May they serve in helping you do the tough and gritty work of leadership.

Zoë Routh, Canberra, 2018

References

1. Barr, S., *Prove It – How to create a high-performance culture and measurable success*, Sydney, Wiley & Sons, 2017.

2. Breuning, L.G., *Habits of a Happy Brain: Retrain Your Brain To Boost Your Serotonin, Dopamine, Oxytocin & Endorphin levels*, Avon, Massachusetts, Adams Media, 2016.

3. Chapman, G.D. and P. White, *The 5 Languages of Appreciation in the Workplace: Empowering Organisations by Encouraging People*, Chicago, Northfields Publishing, 2011.

4. Cook, P., *The New Rules of Management: How to Revolutionise Productivity, Innovation, and Engagement by Implementing Projects That Matter*, Milton, John Wiley & Sons, 2013.

5. Fox, J., *The Game Changer: how to use the science of motivation with the power go game design to shift behaviour, shape culture, and make clever happen*, Milton, Wiley & Sons, 2014.

6. Gladwell, M., *Blink – The Power of Thinking Without Thinking*, London, Penguin, 2005.

7. Kahneman, D., *Thinking, Fast and Slow*, London, Penguin, 2011.

8. Krogerus, M, and R. Tschäppeler, *The Decision Book – 50 models for strategic thinking*, London, Profile Books, 2011.

9. Murphy, P.J. and R.W. Coye, *Mutiny and Its Bounty: Leadership Lessons from the Age of Discovery*, New Haven and London, Yale University Press, 2013.

10. Pink, D., *Drive – The surprising truth about what motivates us*, Edinburgh, Canongate, 2009.

11. Reichheld, F., *The Ultimate Question 2.0 – How Net Promoter Companies thrive in a customer-driven world*, Boston, Harvard Business School Publishing, 2011.

12. Rock, D., *Your Brain At Work: Strategies for overcoming distraction, regaining focus, and working smarter all day long*, Pymble, Australia, HarperCollins, 2009.

13. Routh, Z., *Moments – Leadership when it matters most*, Canberra, Inner Compass Australia Pty Ltd, 2016.

14. Senge, Peter et al., *The Fifth Discipline Fieldbook – Strategies and Tools for Building a Learning Organization*, New York, Doubleday, 1994.

15. Sinek, S., *Start With Why: How Great Leaders Inspire Others To Take action*, London, Penguin Group, 2009.

16. Sinek, S., *Leaders Eat Last – Why some teams pull together and others don't*, London, Portfolio Penguin, 2014.

17. Torbert, B. and associates, *Action Inquiry: The Secret of Timely and Transforming Leadership*, San Francisco, Berrett-Koehler Publishers, Inc., 2004.

Notes